Steve Myers

INFLUEN
Using Myers Briggs

A guide to improving your interpersonal skills and effectiveness, based on the highly popular model of personality, known as Myers Briggs.

Foreword by Dr. Ben Green

Team Technology

British Library Cataloguing in Publication Data..
A catalogue record for this book is available from the
British Library.
ISBN: 0 9526667 0 7
First edition, published in 1995
Second impression

Published and distributed by:
Team Technology
36 Gorse Lane, West Kirby, Wirral, L48 8BH

Printed by:
Wirral Press
Birkenhead

Contents

Foreword

There is a common theme that unites all types of enterprises, whether they be factories, universities, GP surgeries, or high street stores: the well being of these organisations, their profitability and their future, depends on individuals, and how well they work together in teams.

Teams that don't work well together can end up in a state of 'friction' or 'floating'.

Friction occurs where individuals clash. This clash can be overt or, more worringly and more often, covert. Where clashes between individuals lurk beneath the surface, not only does the team fail to realise anywhere near its true potential, but they often fail to accept there is a real problem, and avoid taking the necessary steps required to change.

Floating teams don't clash - they simply fail to communicate on important issues, and float apart. Team members pursue their own objectives and agendas, often at the expense of the team's performance. These teams sometimes dismiss teamwork as 'unnecessary'. Individuals value only their own contribution, and see teamwork as a way of hindering their own 'high standard' of performance.

Both these situations are highly unsatisfactory, from the organisation's and the individual's point of view. The organisation needs people to work together effectively in order to provide a high quality service, and compete in the marketplace. The individual needs to be an effective team member in order to fit in to the 1990s' team culture. Future employment prospects depend as much on the team's performance, and his or her team skills, as individual performance.

To improve team work, 'friction' needs to be reduced, and 'floating' teams need to be anchored. This is where the 'team doctor' can play a role, and help the team to develop the most appropriate strategy. The use of an inappropriate tool can increase friction within a team, or encourage them to float even further apart.

There is a valuable analogy that can be drawn with the General Practitioner. Doctors begin their healing process by undertaking a diagnosis, and then prescribing a recommended treatment. In many cases the cure involves giving up smoking, cutting down the amount of alcohol consumed, or some other change of lifestyle. However, some patients fail to take ownership of a problem that is really theirs, and ask the doctor to 'prescribe some pills' so the problem will go away.

In a similar way, the team doctor needs to perform a diagnosis, to understand the team and decide the nature of the problem. The equivalent of the doctor's pill is the team building workshop - there is a role for it, but it does not absolve the team member from his responsibility. In most cases, a fundamental change of attitude is required, and team members have to work at improving their collective performance and interpersonal skills.

This is where Myers Briggs, and this book, can help you. The doctor's medical training gives him insight into some of the processes taking place within the patient's body. Myers Briggs can provide you with insight into some of the processes taking place in your interpersonal relationships. Understanding your own style, and recognising the personal style of your colleagues, can help you to diagnose some of the problems and decide on appropriate action. This will help you to reduce 'friction', and prevent your team from 'floating' apart.

Steve Myers' book presents the Myers Briggs model in a clever and insightful way. It will help you to:

- recognise the Myers Briggs type in others
- value the strengths of your colleagues, including those who have a somewhat different approach to you
- recognise your colleagues' weaknesses, and understand how to lighten their effect
- become more influential with people of all types, so that you can lead them to personal and team success.

To do all this, you need to start by understanding your own personality type. This book will help you do that, as well.

Dr Ben Green
MB, ChB, MRCPsych.
Consultant in Psychological Medicine and
Editor of The International Journal of Psychiatry
http://www.cityscape.co.uk/users/ad88/psych.htm

1 Introduction

"Myers Briggs" is a way of understanding people.

There are many ways of understanding people, but few are as useful and far-reaching as Myers Briggs. It is based on the teachings of Carl Jung, one of the forefathers of modern psychology, and explains some of the different ways that people think and interact with each other.

These differences, and their application in the work setting, have been supported by extensive research. For example, the Myers Briggs data bank in America holds details of over a quarter of a million people, and that number is growing all the time.

Myers Briggs can provide you with valuable insight into the way that people interact. This insight will enable you to make significant changes to your interpersonal relationships.

Myers Briggs will change your attitude and behaviour towards others, and make your working relationships more productive and enjoyable. It can be used in fields as disparate as:

Developing Communications Skills
Personal Counselling
Career Guidance
Increasing The Effectiveness Of Education Programmes
Marital Counselling
Team Building
Enhancing Sales Skills
And Many More.

This book is designed for anyone whose work involves dealing with people in some way (i.e. everyone). It will help you increase your interpersonal skills, enhance your influence with others, and enable you to add a greater sense of enjoyment to your relationships.

Just reading this book will change your working relationships for the better. If you put some effort into applying the principles contained in it, you will begin to realise the potential that Myers Briggs offers for being more effective in the workplace.

Using Myers Briggs is a bit like playing Othello, which takes "a few minutes to learn, and a lifetime to master". The simple view of Myers Briggs can be grasped in a short time, as it involves just four 'preferences'. However, understanding the dynamic interaction of those preferences, and their implications for everyday work, can take much longer.

Chapter 2 contains an introduction to Myers Briggs. If you are already familiar with the model, you can skip this chapter, or scan through it as revision. If you do decide to skip this chapter, take a quick look at activities 1 to 4 first, as they are referred to later in the book.

Chapter 3 contains some additional information to help you make a provisional estimate of your own Myers Briggs personality type.

Chapter 4 covers some basic interpersonal skills, using the Myers Briggs personality model. This includes a description of behavioural styles that can be observed in the workplace, and leads in to a discussion of how you can modify your style to be more effective with people of particular types.

Chapter 5 covers the most important skill of all - recognising type in others. Not everyone you deal with has completed the Myers Briggs questionnaire, and not everyone who has completed the questionnaire will tell you their type. This chapter will help you to recognise type from observing behaviour.

Chapters 6 and onwards contain a detailed analysis of each of the Myers Briggs types. Use this part of the book to understand the Myers Briggs model in more depth. It can also serve as a handy reference guide when you want to improve your interpersonal relationship with someone whose type you can recognise.

Chapters 2 to 5 contain a number of activities to be done, statements to ponder or questions to answer. You will get the most out of this book if you stop and spend a little time doing these exercises. If you skip them, you may find some of the later parts of the book a little hard to understand.

This book makes random use of "him", "her" and "him/her", in an attempt to avoid any accusations of sexism!

2 An Introduction to Myers Briggs

The Myers Briggs model of personality is based on 4 preferences.

Where is your primary source of energy?

- *From the outer world of activity, and spoken words*

OR

- *From the inner world of thoughts and emotions*

How do you prefer to take in information?

- *In the form of facts and details*

OR

- *In the form of patterns and overviews*

How do you prefer to make decisions?

- *On the basis of logic and objective considerations*

OR

- *On the basis of personal values*

How do you prefer to organise your life?

- *In a structured way, making decisions and knowing where you stand*

OR

- *In a flexible way, discovering life as you go along*

For each of these questions you could probably say 'both answers are true'. For example, at times you perceive information in the form of details, and at other times, in the form of overviews or patterns. At times, your life is organised, and at other times you are more flexible.

The Myers Briggs model does not say that you are constrained to any one type of behaviour. People are very versatile and can exhibit a tremendous variety in the way that they behave. The Myers Briggs model claims, however, that amongst all these behaviours, some are preferred more than others. That is, the Myers Briggs model is based on the concept of preference.

To help understand the implications of exercising 'preference' for behaviour, do the following exercise:

Activity 1 *Hold this book to read, with just one hand.*

As you are reading this paragraph, think about how comfortable it feels to hold the book. Is it a strain? The likely answer is no, and you are wondering about the point of the exercise. Make a mental note of which hand you are using to hold the book.

Activity 2 *Now hold this book with your other hand.*

How does this feel, by comparison with activity 1? The likelihood is that you found a small difference between the two, but readers vary in their strength of preference between holding the booking with the right hand or the left. If you found both hands felt exactly the same, you have demonstrated that you have no clear preference between one hand or the other. However, when asked to hold the book in activity 1, you did choose to use one of your hands - so you exercised a preference of sorts, even though it was a very slight one.

Your experience with the following exercise may be somewhat different.

Activity 3 *Write your name in the following space:*

How did it feel writing your name? Did it feel natural, comfortable, and easy? Is the quality of the result consistent with previous times when you have written your name?

Activity 4 *Now write your name again, but using your other hand:*

How did this feel? Did it feel awkward, cumbersome and hard? How long did it take, by comparison with activity 3? How does the quality of the result compare? Perhaps the quality is better because you put a lot more thought into doing it! If you had to write with your 'other hand' all day, it would probably tire you, and add to your general level of stress.

In these last two exercises you have probably demonstrated a clear preference for one hand over the other. In the first two, there was not a clear preference (though you may have chosen to hold the book with the same hand you write with).

These activities demonstrate the concept of preference. When you have to use your least preferred hand, work can sometimes (but not always) be an effort. You have to think about it more. It takes longer. You get tired more easily. The quality is poor. When you use your preferences, work becomes easier, more enjoyable, better quality, can be done more quickly, etc..

The Myers Briggs model says that each of us has our own preferences for thoughts and behaviour. The same principles of effort and stress apply equally to mental processes as to using your hands. You have the ability to behave in a wide variety of ways, but you are likely to perform at your best when you exercise your preferences. Therefore, it is likely, but not certain, that you tend to behave according to your preferences, just as it is likely that whenever you are asked to sign your name, you will use your preferred hand.

The two sets of exercises you did a few minutes ago also demonstrate that there can be different strengths of preference for doing different things. Your preference for one hand was probably much clearer in the handwriting exercise than in the book holding exercise. Despite this, your particular strength of preference, and also your feelings and experience of doing this exercise, are different from other peoples. Similarly, the way that you behave is different from other peoples. However, just as it is possible to predict most people's reaction to the exercises based on the concept of right and left hand preference, so it is also possible to predict some common themes to people's behaviour based on the concept of Myers Briggs preference.

Understanding your own preferences is an important first step in using Myers Briggs in the workplace to increase your personal effectiveness. We will now look at the four Myers Briggs preferences in more detail, so that you can understand the model, and begin the process of understanding your own preferences.

The first preference - source of energy - E or I

The first preference identifies your primary source of energy - whether it is from the outer world (of actions and spoken words) or from the inner world (of thoughts and emotions). Taking your energy from the outer world is called Extroversion. Taking your energy from the inner world is called Introversion.

During each day you will undoubtedly spend time spontaneously doing or saying things, as well as retreating into the inner world of contemplation and thought. If your working day has involved much interaction with the world, even the clearest Extrovert may feel at the end of the day that he wants to be left alone with his thoughts. Conversely, if an Introvert has been working in isolation all day, she may feel that she needs to 'party' in the evening to restore some balance.

You, like every other individual, need a particular balance of both introversion and extroversion. However, laying aside special circumstances like those in the previous paragraph, one of Extroversion or Introversion will normally increase your level of energy, whilst the other will decrease it.

The following table lists words and expressions that are often associated with extroversion and introversion:

Extroversion	Introversion
social	private
expressive	quiet
many	few
broad	deep
interaction	concentration
outward	inward
action before thought	thought before action

Every individual exhibits all of these characteristics at some time or other. However, what distinguishes an extrovert from an introvert is preferred choice of behaviour. For example, one feature differentiating the two types is whether action or thought comes first.

In situations that demand action, such as the sounding of a fire alarm, both types will act. Most people are trained to evacuate the building immediately in an emergency, or to take other appropriate action. So the fire alarm results in most people doing something, and very few people decide to sit and think.

In situations that demand thought, such as solving a crossword puzzle, both types will think. Most crossword puzzles cannot be solved by taking action or by talking. Both extroverts and introverts need to spend time in thought first, to make some progress towards a solution.

The difference between extroverts and introverts becomes more apparent when there is a free choice. In these situations, the extrovert will tend to act, and the introvert tend to think. However, very few situations involve a truly free choice, as your behaviour (at work, for example) may be influenced by factors such as:

- the culture of the organisation (some employers expect action-oriented behaviour, others expect considered responses)
- your training or upbringing
- a range of environmental factors, such as whether the situation is a new or familiar one, whether recognition or reward is given, and the effects of stress or illness. The need to restore balance may also be a factor (e.g.: an extrovert may need some time alone after a busy week).

Nevertheless, your preferences will influence the way that you behave, as do those factors listed above. In a situation demanding action, an introvert may nevertheless bring a more thoughtful approach, or delay the taking of action. In a situation demanding thought, the extrovert may tend to talk the problem through, or move to action more quickly.

Also, where your preferences coincide with the demands of the situation, you may find it quite enjoyable. An extrovert may find it frustrating if required to work in an introvert style, but enjoyable or energising if required to work in an extrovert style. The introvert may have similar positive feelings when required to work in an introvert style, but find it more difficult when working in extrovert style.

Activity 5 *Looking back to the table describing the differences between extroversion and introversion, which type of situations do you find more enjoyable or energising?*

If you are not sure, that's OK. This is just like being unsure whether you normally hold a book with your right or left hand. You are able to function perfectly well without even thinking about it. Not having a clear preference for your main source of energy is OK. However, coming to understand your preferences can help you, for example, in structuring your work to be more enjoyable.

The second preference - perception - S or N

The second preference is that of taking in information, or perceiving. Do you prefer to perceive in the form of facts and details, or in the form of patterns and overviews? Factually based perception is called Sensing, whilst pattern-based perception is called iNtuition. (The letter N is used to denote iNtuition to avoid confusion with I for Introversion).

Sensing tends to be interested in concrete reality, focusing on the prek-ent, and seeing what is, rather than what might be. At an extreme, Sensing can have its feet so well and truly on the ground that it misses out on possibilities for the future.

The preference for iNtuition gives a greater emphasis on insight and the future, focusing on what might be, rather than what is. At an extreme, iNtuition can focus so much on possibilities that it loses touch with current realities.

Sensing tends to communicate in direct ways, whilst iNtuition prefers to communicate in creative ways.

The following table shows words that are normally associated with each of these two preferences.

Sensing	iNtuition
facts	possibilities
details	overview
present	future
practicality	innovation
enjoyment	anticipation
realism	idealism
using	changing

Activity 6 *Is your preference for Sensing or iNtuition? To help, for each of the pairs of words above imagine newspaper or magazine articles that focus on one word or the other. Tick whichever you would prefer to read. E.g.: if you would prefer to read an article on the possibilities in a situation rather than the facts of a situation, tick possibilities. The column with the most ticks may indicate your preference.*

It is quite normal if you find it difficult to decide whether your preference is for Sensing or iNtuition. At this stage, you are only beginning to learn about the Myers Briggs model, and you may also be just starting to learn about your own preferences. Even when you have learnt more about the model and about yourself, your preference may still not be clear. This can be because you do not have a strong preference - similar, perhaps, to the way in which you feel comfortable using either hand to hold this book.

The third preference - decision making - T or F

The third preference is how you prefer to make decisions. Is it on the basis of logic, using objective considerations, or on the basis of personal values?

Deciding on the basis of objective logic is known as Thinking judgement. This tends to analyse a situation in an impersonal and objective manner, and evaluate the consequences of the various options.

Deciding on the basis of personal values is known as Feeling judgement. This is more subjective, and focuses on what is important to you or to others. It usually takes more account of people's feelings and emotions.

The following table lists words often associated with each of the two preferences.

Thinking	Feeling
analysing	sympathising
objective	subjective
logical	personal
criticism	appreciation
onlooker	participant
decides on principle	decides using values
long term view	immediate view

Activity 7 *How do you prefer to make decisions, on the basis of objective logic, or subjective personal values? To help, tick whichever word, in each pair above, you think is the most admirable quality in a person. The column with the most ticks may indicate which is your preference.*

Remember that there is nothing wrong with not being clear about which is your preference. Everyone makes decisions using both logical consideration and personal values, but the Myers Briggs model states that you will have a preference, even if it is a slight one. That is, in situations where there is free choice, you will tend to use either Thinking or Feeling judgement to make your decisions.

The fourth preference - your lifestyle - J or P

The final preference shows what sort of lifestyle you prefer - organised or flexible. An organised lifestyle is called Judgement, whilst a flexible lifestyle is called Perception.

Someone whose preference is Judgement prefers, in their lifestyle, to make decisions. This means that they prefer to make decisions about what to do, where to go, what to say, and so on. As a result of these decisions, their lifestyle appears organised. That is, someone whose preference is Judgement, prefers to make decisions in the world of actions and spoken words, and therefore appears organised.

Someone whose preference is Perception prefers, in their lifestyle, to learn or experience new things. This means that they prefer to find out more, rather than making decisions, and are more comfortable when they keep their options open. As a result of this openness, they can appear flexible. That is, someone whose preference is Perception, prefers to perceive new things in the world of actions and spoken words, and therefore appears flexible.

Some words often associated with Judgement and Perception are:

Judgement	Perception
close	open
decide	wait
structure	meander
organise	inquire
firmness	flexibility
control	spontaneity

The Myers Briggs model states that your lifestyle is governed either by a preference for deciding (i.e. judgement) or by a preference for or acquiring new information (i.e. perception)

Activity 8 *Do you prefer an organised or flexible lifestyle? To help, ask friends and colleagues to tick, for each pair of words, which one they think characterises you more. The column that contains the most ticks may indicate your preference.*

A Judgement lifestyle tends to be decisive, wanting to bring closure to decisions or resolve ambiguity. Js tend to be well organised and meet their goals by planning ahead. A Perceptive lifestyle is more comfortable with ambiguity, and tends to be flexible and curious, seeking to understand more before making decisions. Ps can therefore appear disorganised, and tend to meet their goals by a last minute rush.

Summary

There are four preferences in the Myers Briggs model.

Where is your primary source of energy?

If it is from the outer world of activity or words, it is called Extroversion, denoted by the letter E. If it is from the inner world of contemplation, or thoughts, it is called Introversion, denoted by the letter I. Extro- is a prefix meaning 'without' and Intro- is a prefix meaning 'within'.

How do you prefer to take in information?
(The Perception preference)

If it is in the form of facts or details, it is called Sensing, denoted by the letter S. If it is in the form of patterns or overviews, it is called iNtuition, denoted by the letter N (N is used to avoid confusion with Introversion). The term Sensing is used because information is taken in primarily by way of the senses. The term iNtuition is used because information is perceived primarily in an intuitive fashion.

How do you prefer to make decisions?
(The Judgement preference)

If it is on the basis of logic and objective considerations, it is called Thinking, denoted by the letter T. If it is on the basis of personal values, it is called Feeling, denoted by the letter F.

How do you prefer to organise your life?

If it is in a structured way, making decisions and knowing where you stand, then it is called Judgement. If it is in a flexible way, discovering life as you go along - this is called Perception. The reasons for these terms being used is a little complicated, and will be covered in a later chapter.

Activity 9 *Indicate, with a tick, which preference each word is usually associated with. Check your answers by referring to earlier sections in this chapter.*

	E	I	S	N	T	F	J	P
open								
sympathising								
possibilities								
many								
deep								
organise								
facts								
criticism								
realism								
appreciation								
decide								
changing								
analysing								
flexibility								
practicality								
values								
control								
interaction								

3 Your Myers Briggs type

Everyone's personality reflects all aspects of the Myers Briggs model. You use Extroversion as well as Introversion, Sensing as well as iNtuition, Thinking as well as Feeling, and Judgement as well as Perception.

However, the Myers Briggs model implies that each person naturally tends to choose, where the opportunity allows, one of each of the four preferences, though the strength of that preference may vary. You have seen examples of varying strengths of preference in the exercises for holding this book with one hand, and writing your name.

The letters that represent your preferences are combined to produced your Myers Briggs Type, such as ENTJ. An ENTJ prefers Extroversion, iNtuition, Thinking and Judgement. The ENTJ is likely to feel energised by having lots of things going on (E). He will tend to interpret events by seeing patterns or overviews (N). He will tend to make decisions on the basis of logic (T). And he organises life on a logical basis (J).

If you have opportunity to complete the questionnaire that is associated with Myers Briggs, it can help you identify what your preferences are. However, like all personality questionnaires, it can on occasion be wrong, and the best judge of your personality type is you.

Activity 10 *List down your own preferences in the four letter form outlined above. If you are unclear about any of them, simply insert a question mark. E.g.: IS?P*

If you have managed to put down four letters with no question marks, regard this as a provisional estimate of your type. You may find it useful to revisit this subject when you have finished reading this book. Even then, you may not be certain, and may find it helpful to read other books that describe the Myers Briggs model. Getting to know your true preferences is a task that can last as little as a few hours, or several months, or even longer.

If you have included two question marks in your own type, that's OK. In some instances, you may find the following list helpful, as it suggests a likely answer to one of those question marks. These are only suggestions - it is important that you come to a conclusion yourself, with which you feel comfortable.

If your guess is:	then consider:
ES?? or EN??	ES?P or EN?P
IS?? or IN??	IS?J or IN?J
?S?P or ?N?P	ES?P or EN?P
?S?J or ?N?J	IS?J or IN?J
E?T? or E?F?	E?TJ or E?FJ
I?T? or I?F?	I?TP or I?FP
??TP or ??FP	I?TP or I?FP
??TJ or ??FJ	E?TJ or E?FJ

The sixteen types

This section contains a brief overview of the sixteen types that result from the Myers Briggs model. Everyone is an individual, but Myers Briggs highlights general themes or similarities between people. Reading this section may help you to consolidate your understanding of the preferences, and help identify your own Myers Briggs type.

ESTJ

The ESTJ takes his energy from the outside world of actions and spoken words. He prefers dealing with facts and the present, and makes decisions using logic. His life is organised on a logical basis. He is therefore practical, and likely to implement tried and trusted solutions to practical problems in a businesslike and impersonal manner. He prefers to ensure that the details have been taken care of rather than spend time considering concepts and strategies.

INFP

The INFP takes her energy from the inner world of thoughts and emotions. She prefers dealing with patterns and possibilities, especially for people, and prefers to make decisions on the basis of personal values. Her life is flexible, following new insights and possibilities as they arise. She is quiet and adaptable (up to a point - when her values are violated the normally adaptable INFP can surprise people with her stance). She will seem to be very interested in ideas, and she may sometimes make very creative contributions. She has a hidden warmth for people and a desire to see self and others grow and develop. She prefers to undertake work that has a meaningful purpose.

ESFP

The ESFP takes his energy from the outside world of actions and spoken words. He prefers dealing with facts, which he usually takes at face value. He also prefers dealing with the present and with people, and probably derives much enjoyment out of friendships. His life is flexible, living it very much in the present, and responding to things as they arise. He is impulsive and friendly, seeking enjoyment out of life, and makes new friends easily. He likes taking part in solving urgent problems, such as fire-fighting or trouble shooting. He operates best in practical situations involving people.

INTJ

The INTJ takes her energy from the inner world of thoughts (and, maybe, emotions). She prefers dealing with patterns and possibilities for the future, and making decisions using impersonal analysis. Her life is organised on a logical basis. She is a strategist, identifying long term goals and organising life to meet them. She tends to be sceptical and critical, both of self and others, with a keen sense of deficiencies in quality and competence. She often has a strong intellect, yet is able to attend to details that are relevant to the strategy.

ESFJ

The ESFJ takes his energy from the outer world of actions and spoken words. He prefers dealing with facts, and making decisions on the basis of personal values. He likes dealing with people, and organises life on a personal basis. He is a very warm person, seeking to maintain harmonious relationships with colleagues and friends, who are a very important part of his life. He can find conflict and criticism very difficult to handle. He has a strong sense of duty and loyalty, and is driven by a need to belong and be of service to people.

INTP

The INTP takes her energy from the inner world of thoughts (and, maybe, emotions). She prefers dealing with patterns and possibilities, and making decisions on a logical basis. Her life is flexible, following new insights and possibilities as they arise. She is quiet and detached, and adaptable (up to a point - sometimes she may stop adapting, insisting that there is a clear principle at stake). She is not interested in routine, and will often experiment or change things to see if they can be improved. She operates at best when solving complex problems that require the application of intellect.

ENFP

The ENFP takes his energy from the outer world of actions and spoken words. He prefers dealing with patterns and possibilities, particularly for people, and makes decisions on the basis of personal values. His life is flexible, following new insights and possibilities as they arise. He is creative and insightful, often seeking to try new ideas that can be of benefit to people. He may sometimes neglect details and planning, but he enjoys work that involves experimentation and variety, working towards a general goal.

ISTJ

The ISTJ takes his energy from the inner world of thoughts (and, maybe, emotions). He prefers dealing with facts, and making decisions after considering the various options. He organises his life on a logical basis. He is quiet, serious and well prepared for most eventualities. He is a keen observer of life, developing a good understanding of situations, which is often not expressed. He has a strong sense of practical objectives, and works efficiently to meet them.

ESTP

The ESTP takes her energy from the outer world of actions and spoken words. She prefers dealing with facts, which she usually views objectively, and she makes decisions on a logical basis. Her life is flexible, consisting of a series of activities that interest her. She is an action oriented problem solver, and prefers to work with practical organisational issues. She can be impulsive, and likes taking part in trouble-shooting-type work. She can sometimes neglect follow-through, but will work best when there is a lot going on that needs organising and solving.

INFJ

The INFJ takes her energy from the inner world of thoughts and emotions. She prefers dealing with patterns and possibilities, particularly for people, and makes decisions using personal values. Her life is organised on a personal basis. She often has a private sense of purpose in life, and works steadily to fulfil that goal. She demonstrates a quiet concern for people, being interested in helping them to develop and grow. She is good at developing insight into people, though it can often remain unexpressed.

ENFJ

The ENFJ takes his energy from the outer world of actions and spoken words. He prefers dealing with patterns and possibilities, particularly for people, and makes decisions using personal values. His life is organised on a personal basis, seeking to develop and maintain stable relationships with those people he likes. He is actively concerned with promoting personal growth in others. He is also highly sociable, and expressive of feelings towards others, but can find conflict and criticism difficult, particularly if it might damage long term relationships. He works best in situations involving people.

ISTP

The ISTP takes her energy from the inner world of thoughts (and, maybe, emotions). She prefers dealing with facts and making decisions on a logical basis. Her life is flexible, demonstrating an interest in acquiring new information that leads to a practical understanding of the way the world works. She is quiet and detached, and adaptable (up to a point). She is often good at solving organisational problems that need to be thought through. She is curious about how and why things work, and can seem impulsive, sometimes producing surprising ideas or doing something unpredictable.

ENTJ

The ENTJ takes his energy from the outer world of actions and spoken words. He prefers dealing with patterns and possibilities, and making decisions after considering the consequences of the various courses of action. His life is organised on a logical basis. He tends to control life, organising systems and people to meet task oriented goals. He often takes the role of executive or director, using a business-like and impersonal approach. He may appear intolerant of people who do not set high standards for themselves or don't seem to be good at what they do.

ISFP

The ISFP takes her energy from the inner world of thoughts and emotions. She prefers dealing with facts and people, and making decisions on the basis of personal values. She is adaptable (up to a point), quiet and friendly. She is interested in people, enjoying their company preferably on an individual basis or in small numbers. She takes a caring and sensitive approach to helping others. She enjoys the present, and tends to dislike confrontation and conflict. She usually acts as a very supportive member of a team.

ENTP

The ENTP takes his energy from the outer world of actions and spoken words. He prefers dealing with patterns and possibilities, and making decisions on a logical basis. He is adaptable, tending to focus on new ideas and interests as and when they arise, particularly if they involve increasing his competence or skill. He is an ingenious problem solver, constantly trying new ideas out, and can seem to enjoy a good argument. He is interested in instigating change, and operates best in overcoming new difficulties where the solution requires the application of creative effort.

ISFJ

The ISFJ takes her energy from the inner world of thoughts and emotions. She prefers dealing with facts and people, and making decisions on the basis of personal values. Her life is organised on a personal basis, seeking to enjoy relationships with people she likes. She is a quiet, serious observer of people, and is both conscientious and loyal. She prefers work that involves being of practical service to people. She is often concerned for and perceptive of how other people feel and dislikes confrontation and conflict

4 Basic Interpersonal Skills

To influence people using Myers Briggs requires an understanding of your own personality type and the type of people with whom you work.

Activity 11 *Identify the Myers personality type of a colleague. Does the Myers Briggs model explain any differences or conflict of style between you?*

There may be one or two people whose personality type you can easily identify. For many people, however, recognising type in others is a difficult skill, and is covered later in this book. For the moment, let us assume that you know your own type, and the type of your colleague. Once you have understood this chapter, you will be in a better position to read 'Recognising Type'.

This chapter will give you some practical ideas for how you can become more effective and influential with that person, using your knowledge of type. It focuses on the style of interpersonal interaction. Each personality type has its own preferred style of behaviour. You can become more influential with another person if you modify your behaviour to accommodate his/her style.

This does not mean that you should try to abandon your own style. On the contrary, in a team environment, your best contribution will be when you are acting according to type. But the lack of compromise of style between individuals destroys team working, whereas accommodating each other's style enhances relationships, improves team performance, and makes everyone's work much more enjoyable.

Extroversion vs. Introversion

The first area where there is potential for a clash of styles is on the preference scale for source of energy. The table below shows some of the main differences between Extroversion and Introversion, as will be manifest in the workplace.

Extroversion	Introversion
Prefers to try things out first, and then think	Prefers to think things through, and then act
Prefers to communicate face to face	Prefers to communicate formal information in writing
Prefers to respond to issues as they come up	Prefers some advanced warning of discussions
Prefers to discuss a broad range of issues	Prefers to discuss a few issues in depth

Activity 12 *Consider two colleagues whose preferences are opposite. What sources of friction might there be in the relationship?*

The following scenario is somewhat of a caricature, but adequately illustrates the types of friction that can result between an Introvert and an Extrovert.

Suppose an Extrovert wishes to resolve an issue that involves an Introvert colleague. She pops her head round the office door of the Introvert and, as he is not in a meeting, starts talking. She prefers to talk things through, and perhaps assumes that because the Introvert does not appear to be busy, he will enjoy a brief interruption.

Immediately, the Introvert's reaction may be one of mild annoyance. The Extrovert may have interrupted important work (i.e.: sorting out issues by thinking them through). He has not been given any advanced notice of the discussion, to allow time to think or prepare. Furthermore, as the discussion develops, the Extrovert goes from topic to topic, causing the Introvert to think on his feet, and discuss subjects in, what he feels is, a superficial manner. Consequently, the Introvert does not feel he has given of his best to the discussion, and may feel annoyed with both the Extrovert and himself.

Later in the day, after he has thought through his own issues, the Introvert decides that he needs to communicate his conclusions to the Extrovert, and therefore sends her a typed memo to arrange a meeting.

When the Extrovert reads the message, she also is immediately annoyed.

The Introvert's office is only 20 feet away, so why doesn't he come and talk to her? The Extrovert can give some immediate feedback, but the Introvert doesn't want a response until 3pm tomorrow, when he wants a meeting just to discuss that one subject! Furthermore, the Introvert will already have come to his conclusions, so there seems little point in having a discussion. What a waste of time, thinks the Extrovert.

This may seem an extreme caricature, but this type of interaction can happen quite frequently, and often unnoticed to the participants. Rather than recognising the differences in personal preferences, colleagues often just experience irritation with each other, and spend time trying to persuade the other to behave more according to his or her own preferences.

Activity 13 *What can you do to be more effective when working with someone whose preference is opposite to yours?*

The most effective approach is to modify your interpersonal style to accommodate the preferences of the individual with whom you are working.

If you are an Introvert, looking to communicate with an Extrovert, then consider trying some of the following suggestions:

- If you can, go and talk face-to-face. If that's not possible, use the telephone. If you have to write, use E-Mail rather than paper, and use short notes.
- Maintain ad hoc, frequent contact - even if it's only to 'touch base' - and have informal discussions in preference to formal meetings (this is also influenced by the J/P preference).
- Be prepared for a discussion that covers a wide range of subjects and don't force the discussion too deeply into one topic.
- Solicit immediate reactions - don't tell the Extrovert to "go away and think about it" and be prepared for the Extrovert to take, or expect, immediate action.
- Allow the Extrovert to think aloud, and develop ideas as he/she is talking. Don't hold him to his expressed thoughts, but allow him to change his mind (particularly P types).

If you are an Extrovert, looking to communicate with an Introvert, then consider trying some of these suggestions:

- Be careful about interrupting the Introvert at his desk - he may be concentrating and sensitive to too many interruptions.
- Give advanced warning of the need to discuss an issue, rather than springing surprises on him. Some introverts may

appreciate having something to read first.

- In meetings, don't introduce too many topics, and be prepared to go more deeply into one subject.
- Don't force the Introvert to take action - allow him time to think about the subject and come to his own conclusions.
- Encourage the Introvert to share his thoughts - don't interpret silence as agreement. The Introvert may still be deciding, but not make this clear to you.
- Some Introverts prefer formal information to be communicated in writing, whilst others prefer dealing with people on a one-to-one basis, particularly those with an F preference.

Using a style appropriate to your colleague is an important first step in being more influential. However, some people may have a concern that this is being 'manipulative'. In fact, when Myers Briggs is used properly, the contrary is true.

The dividing line between influencing skills and manipulation is that, in the latter, you gain at the other person's expense, usually by giving a false appearance. By contrast, when you use Myers Briggs in your interpersonal relationships, you are recognising and respecting your colleague's preferences, and allowing him/her to receive communication in the way that he/she wants. It would be manipulative, for example, if you pretended to be an extrovert if you were really an introvert. However, using Myers Briggs, you can acknowledge and accommodate your differences with a colleague, and practice tolerance.

Sensing vs. iNtuition

The table below shows some of the main differences between Sensing and iNtuition, as will be manifest in the workplace.

Sensing	iNtuition
Prefers to communicate using facts and details	Prefers to communicate the big picture and trends
Proceeds through a project step by step	Uses bursts of energy to address important tasks
Prefers tried and trusted solutions	Prefers to change and innovate
Focuses on the here and now	Focuses on what might be in the future

Activity 14 *Consider two colleagues whose preferences for perception are opposite. What sources of friction might there be in the relationship?*

Consider the following example: a Sensing manager is supervising an iNtuitive in the operation of certain procedures. The iNtuitive will want to change and improve the system, and will initially put much energy into operating the procedures, to learn them. Once this has been done, he then tries to change the procedures. The Sensing manager may object - the previous procedures had worked perfectly well, so why change? In the discussion, the iNtuitive may outline the future benefits of change. This does not convince the Sensing manager, who sees the potential for a workable solution being lost. She gives a list of relevant facts to the iNtuitive, who in turn feels that the Sensing manager is missing the point.

Both Sensing and iNtuition have a contribution to make, but discussions of this nature can result in competition between:

- *continuity and change*
- *realism and idealism*
- *global and local views*

Understanding each others' point of view, and reaching conclusions that keeps both parties happy, will produce a high quality solution. If they don't compromise, the discussion can result in an argument between the principles of continuity <u>or</u> change, rather than a balance of continuity <u>and</u> change.

Activity 15 *How could you become more effective in dealing with people of the opposite preference?*

If you are a Sensing person, looking to communicate with an iNtuitive, consider the following suggestions:

- Describe the overview before the detail
- Discuss the meaning of information or data, and the insight it provides
- Emphasise long term benefits over short term ones
- Discuss the most important steps in a process, in order of importance, rather than going through each step in chronological order.
- Be innovative in your style of communication, and enthusiastic

in your approach
- Identify opportunities and challenges

If you are an iNtuitive, looking to communicate with a Sensing person, then consider the following suggestions:

- Focus on concrete facts
- Discuss the steps involved in the correct sequence
- Emphasise immediate or short-term benefits
- Identify relevant experience or other successful applications
- State the next (practical) step
- If you are outlining an idea, state when the details will be sorted out

You may find that your own preference is so strong that it is difficult to compromise with people of the opposite preference. This is like writing with your other hand (remember the exercise in the introductory section). Alternatively, you may find it easy to operate using the opposite preference. This is like holding the book with your other hand.

How easy it is can depend on how strong your preference is. Whether you find it easy or hard, you will find this form of self discipline rewards you with increased personal effectiveness.

You should also make sure that you have plenty of opportunity to use your own preference as well, or else you may find work becomes very stressful. Accommodating to the other person's type should be a temporary state, not a permanent change.

Thinking vs. Feeling

The table below shows some of the main differences between Thinking and Feeling, as will be manifest in the workplace.

Thinking	Feeling
Is interested in costs and benefits	Is interested in the impact on people
Regards competence as important	Regards others' experience and views as important
Tends to see the flaws in a person or situation	Tends to see the positives in a person or situation
Tends to focus on areas of disagreement	Tends to focus on areas of agreement

Activity 16 *Consider the following combinations of people, and rank them in order of having the most potential for conflict:*
(1) A Thinking person and a Feeling person
(2) Two Thinking people
(3) Two Feeling people

Feeling people tend to avoid conflict. With two people who have Feeling preferences, they are likely to focus on areas of agreement, regard each other's views as important, and consider the impact of what they say on the other. Whilst conflict can arise, particularly if their personal values clash, it is unlikely to do so, or to be openly expressed.

Two Thinking people, on the other hand, will tend to focus on areas of disagreement, and spend time finding the flaws in each other's arguments. This can lead to circular arguments, and an onlooker might observe a lot more conflict than between two Feeling people. However, the two thinkers, having debated the issues, may not feel as if there has been much conflict - they have just used a natural debating style.

An observer is not likely to see much conflict in a Thinking - Feeling relationship. Whilst the Thinker will express criticism and generate conflict, the Feeling person will make efforts to overcome that conflict. However, there is the potential for both to feel dissatisfied with the dialogue. The Thinker may feel that the discussion failed to get going, and that the issues were not adequately debated. On the other hand, the Feeler may take criticism personally, and feel bemused at how the Thinker can be so critical, and then continue the relationship as if nothing had happened.

There is the potential for unconstructive conflict in all three combinations above. The two Thinkers may engage in conflict so much that they fail to spot ways in which they could move forward. The two Feelers may fail to deal with conflict, thereby avoiding issues that need to be addressed. The Thinker and Feeler have potential for resolving conflict constructively and communicating well, providing they can understand each other's position and modify their behaviour accordingly.

For the Thinker, actions that can improve her effectiveness when dealing with a Feeler include:

- Focus on areas of agreement
- Express appreciation for the other person
- Recognise and support the other person's values

- Take a friendly approach
- Identify who else is 'for' the idea
- Demonstrate the positive impact on people
- Be constructive
- Build on proposals rather than criticising others' ideas
- Don't fall into the trap of avoiding conflict or criticism altogether

For the Feeler, actions that can increase his effectiveness when dealing with a Thinker are:

- Be logical in your arguments
- Find out and support the criteria that the thinker uses to evaluate alternative suggestions
- Take a businesslike approach
- Focus on the underlying (logical) principles involved - i.e. the general rules in operation in the situation
- Discuss the costs and tangible benefits
- Don't shirk from conflict

In working relationships, the Feeling person can often increase his personal effectiveness by being more forthcoming with criticism.

Some Feeling people may think that sharing criticism is likely to endanger the relationship. If you are worried about this, talk to your Thinking colleague about it. Start by telling the Thinking colleague that you are trying to develop your ability to manage conflict. Ask how she would feel if you were to give more constructive criticism. Some Thinkers might welcome it!

Recognise that Thinking people are unlikely to modify their views in the absence of feedback from others. Feeling people may not give them that feedback!

Activity 17 *Consider a close working relationship you have with someone. What similarities or differences are there in the way you both react to conflict?*

Judgement vs. Perception

The table below shows some of the main differences between Judgement and Perception, as will be manifest in the workplace.

Judgement	Perception
Prefers to plan work, and then follow the plan	Prefers to tackle work in a flexible manner
Likes to make decisions and then stick to them	Likes to review decisions in the light of new information
Prefers to meet deadlines with time to spare	Prefers to leave things until the last minute
Likes to define boundaries, such as responsibility	Likes to maintain openness

Activity 18 *Consider two people with opposite preferences. What sources of friction are there likely to be in the relationship?*

Such a relationship may lead to, what seems like, a power struggle between the two people, one trying to establish closure, and the other trying to maintain openness. This battle may be manifest in all sorts of areas, such as making decisions, arranging meetings, defining organisational structure, or developing strategy.

There is also a fundamental difference on this scale of how the preferences approach ambiguity. Js seek to resolve ambiguity and bring greater clarity to decisions. Ps are comfortable with ambiguity, and see premature decisions as getting in the way of the important work of exploring the subject further.

Even if both parties agree that a decision needs to be made, there will still be problems of timing. The Judgement person will want to make the decision quickly, whereas the Perception person will want to delay. Also, the Judgement person may well want to establish deadlines that the Perception person is unwilling to accept. The Perception person, given new information, may want to change a decision after it has been made, .

Activity 19 *How could you become more effective in dealing with people of the opposite preference to you?*

If you are a Judging person seeking to communicate with a Perceptive person, consider the following suggestions:

- Adapt to the Perceptive person's agenda, addressing subjects as they arise - don't impose a formal agenda, but explore the subject.
- If new information comes to light, be prepared to review decisions after they have been made.
- Allow the Perceptive person to meet deadlines by a last minute rush.
- Any views you express should be tentative - and can be modified through discussion. This will also be true of the P's views - she should be allowed to change her mind as the discussion progresses.
- When scheduling meetings, leave time free in your diary for the meeting to overrun.

If you are a Perceptive person seeking to communicate with a Judging person, consider the following suggestions:

- Have a clear purpose for the meeting and an agenda that you have both agreed on.
- Adhere to timescales - don't give timescales for events within meetings as this might create anxiety if the other person thinks the meeting is running late.
- Be predictable - if you need to introduce something radically different, give plenty of notice and advanced signals
- Structure the discussion - don't meander through topics. If you do go off at a tangent, make sure you return to the point in the agenda where you left off.
- Focus on reaching decisions and then moving on to the next subject. Don't reopen subjects that have already been concluded.

Summary and review

Differences in preference can be experienced as irritation or tension in the relationship. For those who do not understand the Myers Briggs model, there might not be any obvious cause for this irritation. Where opposite preferences are recognised and can be accommodated, the working partnership often has the potential to achieve far more, as well as being more enjoyable for both parties.

Reduction of tension in a relationship involves four main actions:

- Firstly, become aware of the difference and value of each of the preferences. Awareness of interpersonal style reduces frustration with the other person's behaviour.

- Secondly, get independent feedback from others on your own style, and modify your behaviour to accommodate those of opposite preferences.
- Thirdly, educate the other person about your preferences, and be honest about your own strengths and weaknesses.
- Finally, explore with the other person whether there are any actions that can be taken to accommodate both of your preferences in the working relationship.

This last point is an encouragement to seek a win-win situation. That is, the decisions you reach are acceptable to both of you. Otherwise, you are seeking a win-lose situation, where you want to impose your preferences on the other person. This results in the relationship being a battle. You should stop expecting other people to fit in with your way of working, and start to accommodate them in your own style.

Of course, it can work the other way. You don't want to be in a lose-win situation, where you are yielding all the time to others' preferences. The very nature of win-win is that you both win. If someone is forcing you into a 'lose' position (i.e. making you behave according to his/her preferences rather than yours), you can educate them about the strengths of your personality type. Awareness in the other person of your style can help him to become more tolerant of your approach, and it is a sign of maturity in the relationship if you are able to acknowledge your strengths and your weaknesses. If you are able only to acknowledge your strengths, or only to acknowledge your weaknesses, then you could benefit greatly if you started to focus on the area that has so far been neglected.

Finally, look at the suggestions for communicating in the style appropriate to each preference (they are summarised in the next few pages). For the people you know, some will work and others won't, so try them out to see which ones are effective. The suggestions form a tool kit of ideas, and you should now begin the process of learning when and how to use those tools to greatest effect.

There can often be humour in recognising when a battle of preferences has entered the conversation. This humour can play an important role in diffusing tension, and in reminding both parties to respect the other's position, and reach a point of compromise.

Extroversion summary

Talk Face-To-Face. If Not, Use The Telephone. If You Have To Write, Use E-Mail Rather Than Paper, And Use Short Notes.

Maintain Ad Hoc, Frequent Contact. Have Informal Discussions In Preference To Formal Meetings.

Cover A Wide Range Of Subjects And Don't Force The Discussion Too Deeply Into One Topic

Solicit Immediate Reactions And Be Prepared For The Extrovert To Take, Or Expect, Immediate Action

Allow The Extrovert To Think Aloud, To Develop Ideas As He/She Is Talking And To Change His Mind

Introversion summary

Don't Interrupt The Introvert At His Desk If He Is Deep In Thought. Ask If He Wants You To Come Back Later.

Give Advanced Warning Of The Need To Discuss An Issue, Or Better Still, Give Him Something To Read First.

Don't Introduce Too Many Topics Into The Discussion, And Be Prepared To Go More Deeply Into One Subject.

Don't Force The Introvert To Take Action - Allow Him Time To Think About The Subject And Come To His Own Conclusions.

Encourage The Introvert To Share His Thoughts - Don't Interpret Silence As Agreement.

iNtuition summary

Describe The Overview Before The Detail

Discuss The Meaning Of Information Or Data, And The Insight It Provides

Emphasise Long Term Benefits Over Short Term Ones

Discuss The Most Important Steps In A Process, In Order Of Importance, Rather Than Going Through Each Step In Chronological Order.

Be Innovative In Your Style Of Communication, And Enthusiastic In Your Approach

Identify Opportunities And Challenges

Sensing summary

Focus On Concrete Facts

Discuss The Steps Involved In The Correct Sequence

Emphasise Immediate Or Short-Term Benefits

Identify Relevant Experience Or Other Successful Applications

State The Next (Practical) Step

If You Are Outlining An Idea, State When The Details Will Be Sorted Out And Who Will Do It

Thinking summary

Be Logical In Your Arguments,

Find Out And Support The Criteria That The Thinker Uses To Evaluate Alternative Suggestions

Take A Businesslike Approach

Focus On The Underlying Principles Involved

Discuss The Costs And Tangible Benefits

Don't Shirk From Conflict

Feeling summary

Focus On Areas Of Agreement

Express Appreciation For The Other Person

Recognise And Support The Other Person's Values

Take A Friendly Approach

Identify Who Else Is 'For' The Idea

Demonstrate The Positive Impact On People

Be Constructive

Build On Proposals Rather Than Criticising Others' Ideas

Don't Fall Into The Trap Of Avoiding Conflict Or Criticism Altogether

Judgement summary

Have A Clear Purpose For The Meeting And An Agenda That You Have Both Agreed On

Adhere To Timescales

Be Predictable - If You Need To Introduce Something Radically Different, Give Plenty Of Notice

Keep Track Of Where You Are In The Agenda - Don't Meander Through The Discussion

Focus On Reaching Decisions And Then Moving On To The Next Subject. Don't Reopen Subjects That Have Already Been Concluded.

Perception summary

Adapt To The Perceptive Person's Agenda - Don't Impose A Formal Agenda, But Explore The Subject

If New Information Comes To Light, Be Prepared To Review Decisions After They Have Been Made

Allow The Perceptive Person To Meet Deadlines By A Last Minute Rush

Express Tentative Views, And Be Prepared To Revisit Decisions That Have Already Been Made

When Scheduling Meetings, Leave Time Free In Your Diary For The Meeting To Overrun.

5 Recognising Type

A major assumption of the previous chapter is that you are able to identify the Myers Briggs type of your colleagues. For some, this may be a straightforward matter. However, for many this may be difficult, and this chapter will help you recognise type in others.

In some instances, your colleagues may have completed a questionnaire to find out their type. If you know the result, this may seem to make life easier, but you should also be aware that it could provide you with misleading information.

For example, some individuals are unhappy with the results of the questionnaire after they have completed it - that is, in their view it was inaccurate. One reason for this is the context in which the questionnaire was completed. When it is marked by people working on behalf of your employer, is it any surprise that the result reflects employment expectations rather than personal preferences? Also, the questionnaire can sometimes report 'learned behaviour' rather than your true preference.

The Myers Briggs model is of greatest value when you understand the difference between true preference, and learned behaviour. These differences can be due to cultural influence, upbringing or employment expectations. If you have done the questionnaire, it is worth remembering the following points:

- Questionnaires can be wrong - all respectable questionnaires have been extensively researched to show, on average, how wrong they can be (psychologists call this research 'reliability' and 'validity')
- Completing the questionnaire is the beginning of a process of understanding your preferences better, rather than being a definitive assessment. This learning process can take months or years to complete.
- Only you can decide what Myers Briggs type you are. If the

questionnaire or a psychologist tells you that you are a particular type, you have the right to ignore them and come to your own conclusions.

There are many factors that affect the results of the questionnaire, and you may have found it a little difficult to work out what type you are. It can therefore be very difficult for someone else to work out your personality type! He/she does not know you as well as you do, nor have they seen you in as many disparate situations as you have. However, someone else does have the advantage of having a more objective viewpoint, and an independent observer can sometimes be aware of things about yourself that you are not. Nevertheless, observing type in others requires a good understanding of the model, practice at the skill of recognising type, and much more information than can be given just by the questionnaire.

This chapter will describe a number of techniques that will help you to recognise the Myers Briggs type in other people. The first of these involves observing the individual and noting what types of behaviours you see most frequently. You will see behaviour that is consistent with all eight of the preferences, but it is the frequency of that behaviour that often indicates the person's type. If someone is out partying for five nights a week, and spends two nights quietly at home, the evidence would suggest he is an extrovert.

Observing type in others can take a long time and will need prolonged exposure to the person. Everyone has a number of different personae that they use in different situations. For example, the form of dress used for work is often different from that used at home, socially, at church, etc.. Similarly, behaviour often varies from situation to situation. Each individual therefore has multiple identities, which is perfectly normal, and does not indicate any psychological problem.

The tables on the following pages give a summary of the types of behaviour often associated with each preference.

Extroversion	Introversion
actively seeks involvement in social activities	actively seeks privacy
is expressive of thoughts, and tends to think aloud	keeps his thoughts to himself, and can be quiet
tends to get involved in many tasks	tends to focus on a few tasks
takes a broad perspective in discussions	explores subjects to some depth
tends to interact with people and the environment	tends to concentrate on the issue in hand
has an outward focus, on other people or things	has an inward focus, sometimes wrapped up in own thoughts
tends to act or speak first, and then think later	tends to think first, and then act or speak
communicates where possible by face to face discussion	communicates formal information in writing
enjoys responding to issues as they come up	prefers some advanced warning of discussions

Sensing	iNtuition
prefers dealing with concrete facts	enjoys exploring abstract ideas and possibilities
likes information to be presented in the form of details	prefers to be given an overview or the big picture
focuses on the present and enjoys things as they are	looks towards the future to achieve something better
takes a practical approach to life, trusting experience	contributes creative ideas, following his inspiration
proceeds in a sequential or step-by-step fashion	proceeds in a random fashion, missing out 'unnecessary' steps
is a realist - at extreme with her feet stuck on the ground	is an idealist - at extreme, with his head in the clouds
tends to use things for the purpose they were intended	tends to change things to be better or do something new
sets goals that are specific about what is to be achieved	sets goals that are general and reflect the underlying purpose
prefers tried and trusted solutions	prefers to invent his own solutions

Thinking	Feeling
tends to analyse a situation	tends to sympathise with those in a situation
takes a logical and objective approach	takes a personal and subjective approach
tends to criticise or see the flaws in situations	tends to appreciate or see the positive in situations
can be detached, as if an onlooker to the situation	feels involved as a full participant in the situation
decides by identifying the principles involved	decides by reference to personal values
tends to take a long term view	tends to take an immediate view
focuses on the differences in people's arguments	tries to find agreement during discussions
is interested in costs and benefits	is interested in the impact on people
regards competence as important	regards others' experience and views as important

Judgement	Perception
defines boundaries and establishes closure	leaves things loosely defined and maintains openness
establishes a structure to life	takes life as it comes
organises people and/or things	learns about or experiences people or things
tends to take a firm approach	tends to take a flexible approach
seeks to control self and others	seeks to act spontaneously
plans work, and then follows the plan	tackles work in a flexible or casual manner
makes decisions quickly and then sticks to them	postpones decisions, or reviews them after they're made
prefers to meet deadlines with time to spare	leaves things until the last minute
prefers clarity to ambiguity	sees clarity as sometimes restrictive

Recognising Type

In Myers Briggs terms, a manager may find that she behaves as an ESTP in work, because the work involves trouble shooting and requires tough decision making. Yet, at home, the person may behave as an ISFJ, which (we shall suppose for this example) is her true preference.

Activity 20 *If this ESTP/ISFJ manager were to complete a Myers Briggs questionnaire at work, what might the result be?*

The result of the questionnaire might be ISFJ, ESTP, a combination of the two (e.g.: ISTJ), or an unclear result, depending on the level of self-awareness of the individual and the context of the test. For example, if the questionnaire was completed on an assessment or development centre, the result may be ESTP. She might answer the questionnaire in a way that avoids reflecting badly on her in a work context (this may be done either consciously or subconsciously).

Sometimes it is difficult for the individual to understand his/her own preferences. This can make it more difficult for others to see his/her type. On the other hand, to an objective observer who knows the person both socially and in work, the disparity between the two personas is often obvious, and the natural style of the person may also seem clear. At work, however, you often observe a person within one role only. Deciding on someone's type on the basis of a single situation can be very difficult, especially where there is a strong employment culture.

One way to be able to recognise type in others is

- to build up an understanding of the model, and the behaviours associated with each preference, perhaps using the tables on pages 36-39 as a reminder.
- to observe an individual in as many different settings as possible, and build up a composite picture of behavioural clues
- to match the behavioural clues to the model, and come to a provisional conclusion about type. You may need to review your decision as you get to know the person better.

A difficulty you may run across when using this approach is that there may seem to be many conflicting clues about behaviour. If you observe a person closely, you may see behaviour that supports all eight of the preferences. Sorting out these conflicting clues is an important task when trying to recognise type in others.

Behaviour vs. Preference

The Myers Briggs model reflects preferences, but does not necessarily dictate behaviour. Everyone uses all kinds of behaviours at some time or other. However, the preferred behaviour is likely to be used more often, be more enjoyable, and be the more 'natural' response in a situation. Recall the handwriting and book-holding exercises in the first chapter.

Activity 21 *How can you tell whether someone is right or left handed?*

In simple terms, you would observe his behaviour and see whether he uses his right or left hand most often. You would take account of which hand produces the better quality result, and whether he is more relaxed using his right or left hand, etc..

However, the situations that you observe are critical. If he is driving a car, he will 'prefer' to use his left hand for changing gear (in the UK!). However, this is not an exercise of preference, but behaviour forced upon him by circumstances - right-handed cars have the gear lever on the left so there is no free choice. When reading a book, the choice of hand may not be significant. However, some behaviours clearly encourage the use of the preferred hand, such as writing, using scissors, a sports racquet, etc..

In the same way, you need to be aware of the influence of the social setting on the individual's behaviour. In a department of auditors, you are likely to see a lot of attention to detail. In a marketing agency, you may see a lot of extroversion displayed. These may be cultural demands, rather than personal preferences. However, people with particular preferences often choose to go into occupations that require their natural type of behaviour. Hence, Introverted Sensing people (IS-- types) are more likely to be auditors than Extroverted iNtuitives (EN-- types), who are more likely to work in marketing. The point here is that you have to distinguish between preference, and behaviour demanded by the social setting.

Misleading behaviour!

Another point to note about behavioural clues is that there are some behaviours that can arise from more than one preference. You could be misled into thinking that you have seen evidence of one preference, but the behaviour actually results from another. For example:

- A behavioural trait of 'liking to be with people' could result from Extroversion or Feeling. This liking for being with people may be exaggerated by the preference for Sensing (wanting to enjoy others' company).

- Attention to detail can arise from Sensing or Thinking (where the detail results from the logical organisation). This can be exaggerated by the preference for Introversion (where more time is likely to be spent in thinking the details through). Judgement can also provide a focus on detail, as it is more concerned with completing the process than Perception.
- A disorganised lifestyle is normally associated with the preference for Perception, but iNtuitives can also appear somewhat disorganised, even when their preference is for Judgement. The appearance of disorganisation may also be exaggerated by Extroversion (which likes to have many things 'on the go') and Feeling.

When looking for behavioural clues, therefore, be mindful that some behaviours can result from several of the preferences.

Activity 22 *Consider the Introvert preference for communication of formal information in writing. Which of the other preferences might counter this, such that the individual does not prefer written communication?*

For an F, interpersonal contact is usually more important than a T. So an I-F- type may prefer to communicate by talking to someone on a one-to-one basis, because paper gets in the way of personal contact. However, the I-T- type may prefer information to be more objective, and have some logical structure, which is often best achieved on paper. The preference for Sensing may also combine with the preference for Feeling to produce a real enjoyment of dealing with people. Therefore, an ISFJ or ISFP may prefer to communicate orally rather than in writing. Other Introvert types, such as ISTJ, may feel more comfortable with paper.

In summary, we have learnt that recognising type is based on observing the types of behaviours that you most frequently see in an individual, especially in situations where there is free choice and no cultural pressure (typically that means away from the work environment). These behaviours give clues that you can evaluate to help recognise type in others.

Training

Personal preferences and the demand of the job are not the only influence on an individual's behaviour. Upbringing and training also influence what an individual says or does. Where the training is ingrained, it is quite possible that someone's preferences may be of one Myers Briggs type, yet the most frequent behaviour that is observed, in situations of free choice and no apparent cultural pressure, is of another type.

In this case, how can you tell what is the Myers Briggs type? Here are some suggestions to help you distinguish between learned behaviour and true preference:

- Observe an individual in as many different contexts as possible, including: a variety of work and social settings; with subordinates, peers and superiors; and with children and adults. It is perfectly normal for behaviour to differ greatly between different situations, but you will observe common themes.
- Work out what is the cultural 'norm', and then observe to which side of that norm the person's behaviour is. For example, in a highly Extrovert environment, everyone, including the Introverts, will be accustomed to working in groups. However, you may see Introverts spend less time in groups than the Extroverts, or they may be less enthusiastic about participating.
- Observe how the behaviour and situation affects the person. Increased stress results from using behaviours that do not fit in with one's preference. Using preferences will result in reduced stress and a greater enjoyment of life.

Distinguishing learned behaviour from true preferences is a difficult task, and for the purpose of 'influencing skills', it is not an area that needs much attention. However, if you are interested in it for your own personal development, read 'Navigating Mid-life', the details of which are given at the end of this book.

Classic Temperament

Another aid to recognising type is to look for the 'classic temperaments'. These are the four types of people that were first observed by Greek philosophers 2,500 years ago. This book gives you a brief overview of the temperaments. If you are interested in more information, then read 'Please Understand Me', details of which are at the end of this book.

When trying to recognise type, you will see a flavour of all four temperaments in everyone. However, one will be more important to the individual than the others, and this may give a clue as to Myers Briggs type. The four temperaments are:

- The Apollonian or Choleric temperament. He/she is driven by a search for meaning or purpose, and therefore seeks to do work that has some worth or value. This type is iNtuition and Feeling (-NF-).
- The Promethean or Phlegmatic temperament is driven by a search for competence, quality or excellence, and therefore is constantly seeking to improve how well a job is done. This type is iNtuition and Thinking (-NT-).
- The Dionesian or Sanguine temperament is driven by a desire to be free from constraint, and to experience and enjoy life. A Dionesian seeks to enjoy work, is often impulsive and doesn't like being closely supervised. This type is -S-P.
- The Epimethean or Melancholic temperament is driven by a need to belong, to be of service and fulfil duty. The Epimethean is often keen to do the right thing, be involved in what is going on, and ensure that others are happy with the service provided. This type is -S-J.

Myers Briggs - the dynamic model

Another way to recognise type is to look at the individual using the 'dynamic' view of Myers Briggs. So far, we have looked at Myers Briggs in terms of four preferences:

- Where is your source of energy?
- How do you prefer to perceive information (the Perception preference)?
- How do you prefer to make decisions (the Judgement preference)?
- Do you prefer your lifestyle to be organised or flexible?

Recognising type has so far involved looking for behaviours that indicate the individual preferences of the individual, which is the 'simple' view of Myers Briggs. This view can sometimes be insufficient to recognise type in others, as people use behaviours from all eight preferences. The dynamic model provides you with an alternative way of viewing Myers Briggs, that, once mastered, makes it a lot easier to recognise type.

You have already had a hint of the 'dynamic' model, when considering the fourth preference - an organised or flexible lifestyle. You may recall the terms 'Judgement' and 'Perception' and wonder why they were used to describe organised and flexible lifestyles. There is actually a very good reason!

You may have noticed that these words - Perception and Judgement - are similar to the second and third preferences. The second preference is concerned with how you acquire information (Perception), and the third is concerned with how you make decisions (Judgement).

Your preference for perceiving (which is Sensing or iNtuition) is used primarily in EITHER the outer world of actions and spoken words, OR the inner world of thoughts and emotions.

Similarly, your preference for judging (which is Thinking or Feeling) is also used in either the outer or the inner world, whichever world is OPPOSITE to the one in which the Perception function operates.

Therefore, your preference for Perception operates primarily in one world, and the preference for Judgement operates primarily in the other. That is, of the middle two letters of the Myers Briggs type, one operates in the inner world, and the other in the outer world.

Activity 23 *If, in an INTJ, the preference for iNtuition operates mainly in the inner world, which preference operates mainly in the outer world?*

For this type of question, you should focus on the middle two preferences (N and T). N operates in the inner world, so T operates in the outer world. That is, as iNtuition operates mainly in the inner world, the Thinking preference will operate mainly in the outer world.

Activity 24 *If, in an ESTP, the preference for Thinking operates mainly in the inner world, which preference operates mainly in the outer world?*

The middle two letters are S and T. T operates in the inner world, so S operates in the outer world.

So, for every Myers Briggs type, the model states that one of the middle two letters operates in the outer world, and the other in the inner world. But which one?

The answer is given by the fourth preference, which simply states which of the middle two preferences is used in the outer world. If the last letter is a J, then the judging preference operates in the outer world - that is, the 3rd letter. If the last letter is a P, then the perceiving preference operates in the outer world - that is, the 2nd letter. In summary:

- If J, then the 3rd letter (T or F) operates in the outer world

- If P, then the 2nd letter (S or N) operates in the outer world.

Activity 25 *For an INFP, which preference operates in the outer world, and which operates in the inner world?*

The fourth letter is a P, so it points to the second preference as operating in the outer world, that is: N. This means that F operates in the inner world.

Activity 26 *For an ESTJ, which preference operates in the outer world, and which in the inner world?*

The fourth preference is a J, so it points to the third preference as being in the outer world, that is: T. Therefore, S operates in the inner world.

Activity 27 *For each of the types below, work out which preference operates in the outer world, and which operates in the inner world.*

	Inner	Outer
ESFP		
INFJ		
ISTP		
ENTJ		

The correct solutions are: ESFP = F (inner) and S (outer);
INFJ = N and F;
ISTP = T and S;
ENTJ = N and T.

To sum up so far, the Myers Briggs model states that your lifestyle (i.e. the outer world of actions and spoken words) is governed either by your preference for deciding (i.e. T or F judgement) or by your preference for acquiring information (i.e. S or N perception). It is the fourth preference that tells you which, by stating, simply, Judgement or Perception.

The order of functions

We have now started to explore the dynamic view of Myers Briggs. We have seen that the fourth preference focuses attention on the middle two preferences - perceiving and judging. These middle preferences - Sensing, iNtuition, Thinking and Feeling - are called 'Functions', and as an individual you have, and use, all four functions. At various times throughout the day, you will perceive by Sensing, and by iNtuition, and you will make decisions using logic, and using personal values.

We have also seen that, of these four functions, you prefer to use two of them - one perceiving function and one judging function.

The dynamic view of Myers Briggs also states that you exercise a preference between the perceiving function and the judging function. That is, one of these is preferred more than the other. For example, we already know that an NF type prefers iNtuition over Sensing, and Feeling over Thinking. However, she also exercises a preference between iNtuition and Feeling.

This leads to an overall order to the four functions - one is most preferred, there is then a second choice, then a third, and finally the least preferred.

Activity 28 *In the handwriting, and holding the book exercises, you used your*

(a) right hand to write
(b) left hand to write
(c) right hand to hold the book and
(d) left hand to hold the book.

Rank these into order, by clarity of preference. That is, which of these do you prefer most? Which is second? Etc.

You may have concluded with a result such as:

- *Most clear preference = (a) Right hand to write*
- *2nd most clear preference = (c) Right hand to hold the book*
- *3rd = (d) Left hand to hold the book*
- *Least preferred = (b) Left hand to write*

You probably found your first choice easy, as you clearly choose to use one hand for writing, and this preference is consistently exercised throughout your life. Consequently, the least preferred was probably also clear - you never choose to write with your other hand, only doing so when you are forced to by circumstances. However, you may not have been so sure about the others, as you may not exercise much preference between holding the book with your right hand or your left.

In a similar way, there is a hierarchy of preference for the four functions, where one is most preferred, and the opposite of that preference is the least preferred. For example, if the most preferred function is iNtuition, then the least preferred function is always Sensing, and Thinking and Feeling make up the second and third preferences. The following table shows the order of preferences for each Myers Briggs type:

Myers Briggs type	Order of preference of functions			
	1st	2nd	3rd	4th
ENFP or INFJ	N	F	T	S
ESTP or ISTJ	S	T	F	N
ENTJ or INTP	T	N	S	F
ESFJ or ISFP	F	S	N	T
ENTP or INTJ	N	T	F	S
ESFP or ISFJ	S	F	T	N
ESTJ or ISTP	T	S	N	F
ENFJ or INFP	F	N	S	T

This order of functions is reflected in your approach to problem solving. An ENFP is likely to start to solve a problem by using the iNtuition function. That is, he is likely to ask: What are the possibilities in this situation? What is the vision? Where is this leading to? Is there anything that can be changed?

The most likely second step in the process is to use the Feeling function, considering the impact on people and other personal values. The ENFP will choose a possibility that fits in with what he wants to do, has a positive impact on people who are important to him, and does not violate any of his values.

The next most likely step (if it gets this far) is to use the Thinking function, and reject any solution that is too costly or does not provide the appropriate benefits.

Finally, the ENFP may investigate the facts, to see if they are consistent with the chosen solution.

The order of functions for an ENFP can therefore be represented by the following diagram:

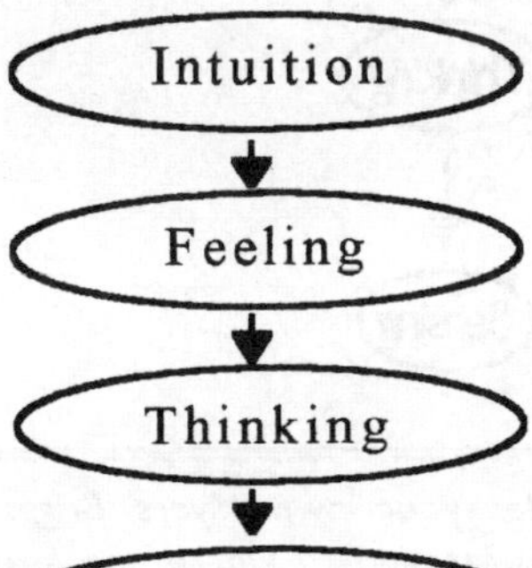

Dominance

The order of preferences obviously means that one function is preferred far more than the others. As you can clearly see from the handwriting exercise, you use your preferred hand much more than your other hand. Similarly, you normally use your most preferred function far more than the least preferred.

The most preferred function is sometimes called the dominant. In most circumstances, you use the dominant function more than any of the others, and your personality is therefore dominated by it. The dominant function of an ENFP is iNtuition. An ENFP is therefore 'dominated' by the characteristics associated with iNtuition - change, variety, the future, possibilities, patterns, insight, etc.. The diagram showing the hierarchy of functions can be redrawn by using the size of the ellipse to reflect how much the function is used. For an ENFP, the diagram might therefore appear as overleaf:

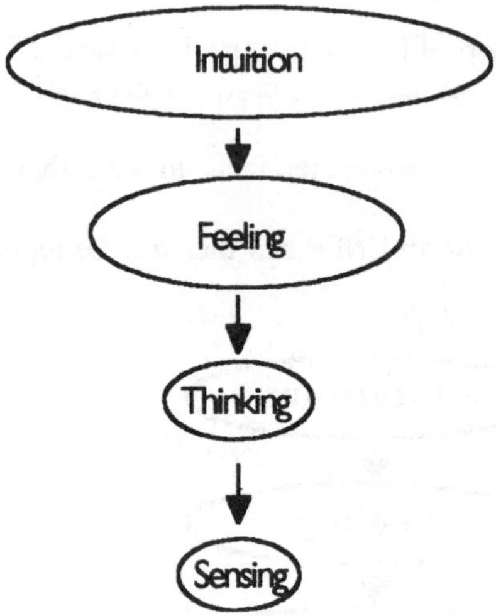

Activity 29 *Consider your own Myers Briggs type. Draw a diagram, as above, where the sizes of the ellipses reflect how much you use that function (if necessary, refer back to the table on page 48 showing the order of preference of functions). Make a note of the characteristics normally associated with your dominant function.*

Interactions between functions

The character of an individual is dominated by the dominant function. However, the dominant function does not operate in isolation from the other functions, and the way in which the dominant expresses itself is influenced by the function chosen as second preference. This is normally called the auxiliary.

For example, the ENFP's dominant is iNtuition, which perceives information in the form of patterns and possibilities. The way that this preference for insight is expressed is influenced by the Feeling function, which has an interest in people, and things of importance to the individual. The ENFP, therefore, prefers perceiving patterns and possibilities in people and other things that have meaning.

By contrast, an ENTP has a dominant function of iNtuition, and an auxiliary function of Thinking. Thinking is interested in logic, and principles. Thinking will therefore influence the iNtuitive function to perceive patterns and possibilities that help understand the theoretical basis of how and why things work. The ENTP's interest is therefore more likely to be in the sciences than in people, though people can sometimes be interesting subjects for scientific study.

The diagram of the functions for the ENFP can now be redrawn to show them as an integrated whole, to reflect both the order of functions and their interaction.

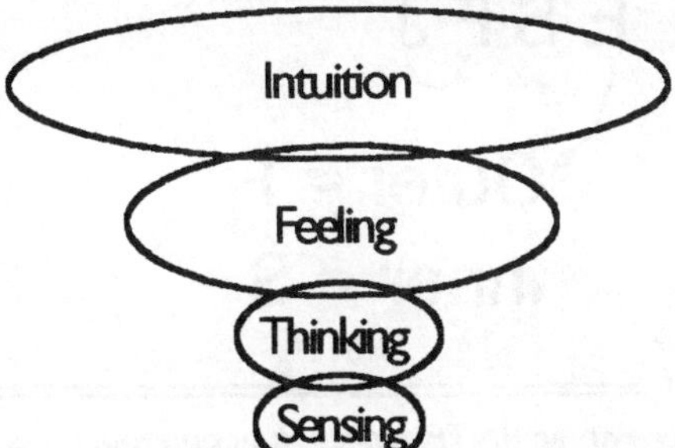

Activity 30 *Consider your own Myers Briggs type. How might your dominant function be influenced by your auxiliary function?*

This is a hard question to answer at this stage, and if you've had a go at it - well done! You can find a detailed answer in the chapter that is dedicated to your type later in this book.

Whilst the most preferred function is called the Dominant, the second most preferred is called the Auxiliary, the third preferred function is called the Tertiary, and the least preferred is called the Inferior.

In which world is the dominant?

The first preference (Extroversion vs. Introversion) states in which world the dominant function operates. Extroversion means that the dominant operates mainly in the outer world, whilst Introversion means that the dominant operates mainly in the inner world.

Activity 31 *In an ESFJ, which function operates in the outer world, which operates in the inner world, and which is the dominant?*

J points to the third preference as being in the outer world, which is F. So S operates in the inner world.

The first preference is E, so the dominant is in the outer world. The outer world function is F, so F is the dominant.

The diagram overleaf may help to explain this.

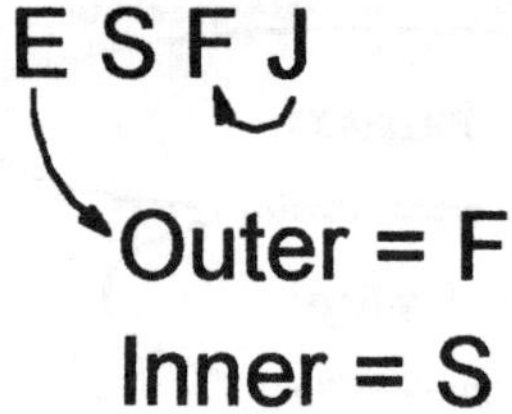

Activity 32 *For an INTP, which function operates in the outer world, and which in the inner? Which function is dominant?*

The last preference is P, which points to iNtuition being in the outer world. Thinking is therefore in the inner world.

The first preference points to the inner world, to find the dominant. The inner world is governed by Thinking, so Thinking is the dominant.

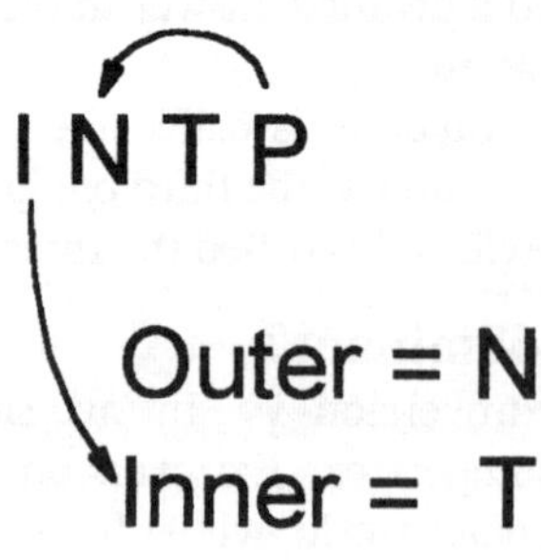

Activity 33 *Work out the inner and outer functions for the following types and then place a circle around the dominant function:*

Inner | Outer

ESTP

INTP

ENTJ

ISFJ

The answers are: ESTP = T inner, S outer and dominant;
INTP = T inner and dominant, N outer;
ENTJ = N inner, T outer and dominant;
ISFJ = S inner and dominant and F outer.

To recap, the fourth preference shows whether it is the perceiving function or the judging function that operates in the outer world. The first preference shows whether the dominant function is used primarily in the outer world of actions and spoken words, or the inner world of thoughts and emotions.

We shall now consider what difference it makes to behaviour if the dominant operates in the outer world or the inner world.

How is behaviour affected by this?

The outer world consists of actions and spoken words, that the individual spontaneously expresses. The inner world consists of thoughts and emotions that the individual is aware of, but does not express (spontaneously) to the world.

Therefore, a preference for Extroversion (i.e.: the dominant function operates mainly in the outer world) means that the person prefers to spontaneously express themselves, as well as derive energy from what is going on outside.

A preference for Introversion (i.e. the dominant process operates mainly in the inner world) means that the person prefers to think and feel without spontaneous expression, and those thoughts and feelings provide the Introvert with energy. With an Introvert, there can be a lot going on inside that the world is not aware of.

An extrovert who uses her preference for judgement to govern her lifestyle will use judgement in the outer world of actions and spoken words. She will speak in terms of decisions, and will act out those decisions. She will therefore appear decisive, and organised.

If the preference is for Thinking judgement, her life will be logically organised. If the preference is for Feeling judgement, her life will be organised around things or people that are important to her. Whether it is Thinking or Feeling, the preference for an organised lifestyle is called Judgement, as a reminder that being organised results from using the preference for judgement to govern daily life.

An extrovert who uses her preference for perception to govern her lifestyle applies perception to actions and spoken words. For example, she may be interested in learning through doing or talking. In fact, she is more interested in learning than being decisive (at least, this is how it appears to other people). She may therefore appear inquisitive and flexible.

If the preference is for Sensing perception, her life will be focused on acquiring facts or experiencing and enjoying life as it is. If the preference is for iNtuitive perception, her life will be focused on changing things for the better and promoting insight. Whichever of these is chosen, the preference for a flexible lifestyle is called Perception, as a reminder that being flexible results from using the preference for perception to govern daily life.

Activity 34 *Think about an extrovert who primarily uses his preference for Feeling judgement (i.e. deciding on the basis of personal values) to govern his lifestyle. Will his life be organised or flexible? Make a note of what characteristics his lifestyle will have.*

Such a person values people, is decisive, and applies that decisiveness to actions and spoken words. Other people are often important to FJ types, so he will do and say things to encourage others, and to build harmonious relationships with them. He is more likely to state his values than keep them to himself and he will organise his life to conform to those values. He may find some situations difficult if these efforts to organise life are thwarted - e.g. if someone he admires spurns any attempts at friendship.

Activity 35 *Think about an extrovert who primarily uses her preference for Sensing perception (i.e. acquiring information in factual form) to govern her lifestyle. Will her life be organised or flexible? Make a note of the characteristics you think her life might have.*

Her sensing is applied to actions and spoken words, so she will do and say things that are concerned with facts, the present, enjoyment and realism. She may therefore enjoy visiting new places, or taking part in sports, to experience them and enjoy them. As new opportunities present themselves, it is likely that she would seek to enjoy these also. As she is not too concerned about applying decisiveness, she would therefore appear flexible, perhaps turning from one interest to another. She may not complete activities once the interest in them has passed.

Let us now return to the ongoing example of the ENFP that we have considered earlier in the chapter.

For the ENFP, the outer world is managed primarily by the iNtuition function (as the 4th preference is P for Perception, and the 2nd preference is N). The dominant function operates in the outer world, as the 1st preference is E. So the dominant function is iNtuition, and it is used primarily to manage the outer world. That is, the characteristics of iNtuition are applied primarily to actions and spoken words.

In an introvert such as an INFJ, the characteristics of iNtuition are applied primarily to the inner world of thoughts and emotions.

Activity 36 *One feature of iNtuition is change. What are the differences between use of iNtuition in the outer world, and use of iNtuition in the inner world?*

In the extroverted form, change would be applied to the outer world of actions or words. The iNtuitive is therefore like to do or say something to create change. She is likely therefore to experiment with ideas, to change something, be creative, suggest an idea for change, or find some other way that spontaneously expresses her preference for change. This is called extroverted iNtuition.

In introverted form, the change is likely to be applied to the inner world of thoughts and emotions. The iNtuitive is therefore likely to think or feel differently. He will constantly be revising his insight into the world, seeking to develop a greater understanding or better vision of the future.

Therefore, the extroverted iNtuitive seeks primarily to change the world to fit his understanding or ideas, whilst the introverted iNtuitive seeks to change his understanding and ideas to fit the world.

Activity 37 *If iNtuition in the ENFP is extroverted, which function is mostly used in the inner world of thoughts and emotions, and which is dominant?*

In the ENFP, Feeling is introverted (i.e.: used in the inner world of thoughts and emotions), and the extroverted iNtuition is dominant.

The diagram for the ENFP can be revised again, to split the use of the functions between the inner and outer world, to show where each of the functions is mostly used.

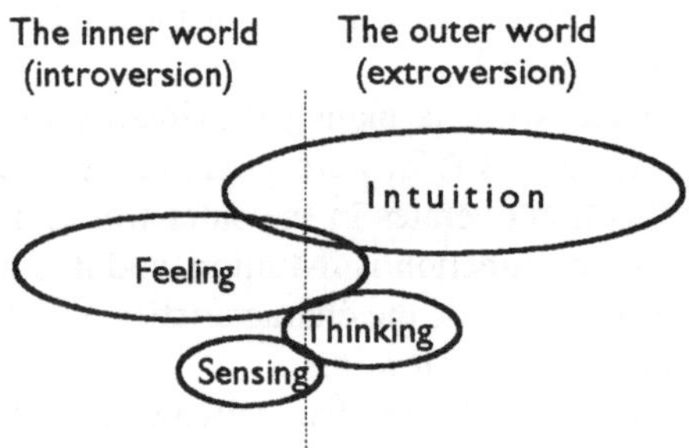

This is the final version of the diagram.

In this diagram, the Thinking function has been shown in the outer world, and the Sensing in the inner world. The least preferred function (in this case, Sensing) is believed to operate mainly in the world opposite to the dominant. There is some controversy as to the normal pattern for extroverting or introverting the tertiary (in this case, Thinking). Some people believe that the tertiary operates in the same world as the dominant, others believe it operates in the opposite world, and yet more others believe it can operate in either. In my view, this is a dynamic model, where each function operates to some degree in both the outer and inner worlds - so it is not too important to resolve this issue.

Having said that, the extroversion of Thinking in this case can explain some potential anomalies and misunderstandings. Whilst the ENFP is primarily a Feeling person, others may perceive him or her as being logical first. Suppose there is a significant cultural pressure, within the business environment, to operate in a logical fashion. As other people's views affect the individual's view of himself, he may come to believe that he is more logical, and lose touch with the inner Feeling side. (This issue might be raised during the 'mid-life transition', when individuals often seek to understand themselves better, and pay more attention to their own needs rather than accommodating the cultural pressure on them to conform. For further discussion of this subject, see 'Navigating Mid-life', listed at the end of this book in 'Recommended Literature'.)

Later in this book, in the chapters that provide a detailed analysis of each type, the diagram has been drawn to show the tertiary function as in the same world as the dominant - but it could be either.

You should also be aware that this particularly style of diagram is a new way of representing the Myers Briggs functions, so you may not come across it anywhere else. However, it accurately reflects all that is contained within the Myers Briggs model, and enables a complicated subject to be simplified in an easy to understand visual form.

How to draw the diagram

There now follows a detailed description of how to draw the diagram for any Myers Briggs type, from the four letter code. The instructions will be illustrated using the example of ENFP, that we have already been discussing.

Follow the steps outlined:

1. *Draw a dotted line down the centre of the page, and put the headings Introversion or the inner world at the top left, and Extroversion or the outer world at the top right.*

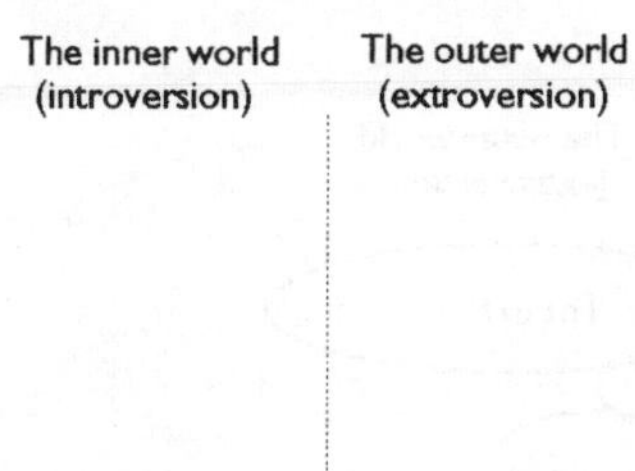

2. *If the first letter is E, draw a large ellipse below Extroversion. If the first letter is I, draw the ellipse under Introversion.* For the

ENFP, it is extroversion:

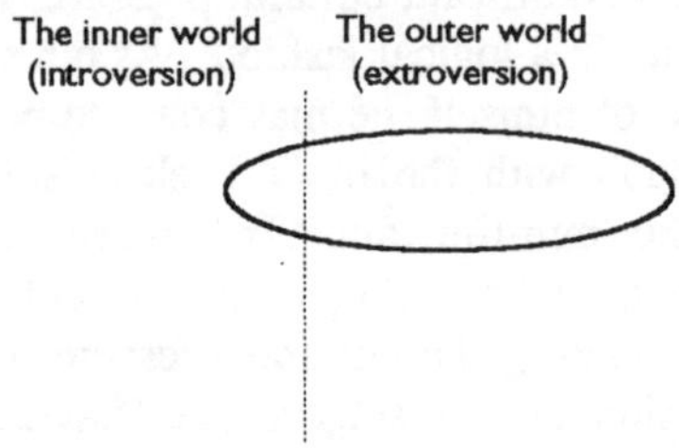

3. *Draw the remaining ellipses, alternating between introversion and extroversion, and making the ellipses smaller as you go down the page.* You will see that in each column there are two ellipses, the top one is bigger than the bottom one in each column.

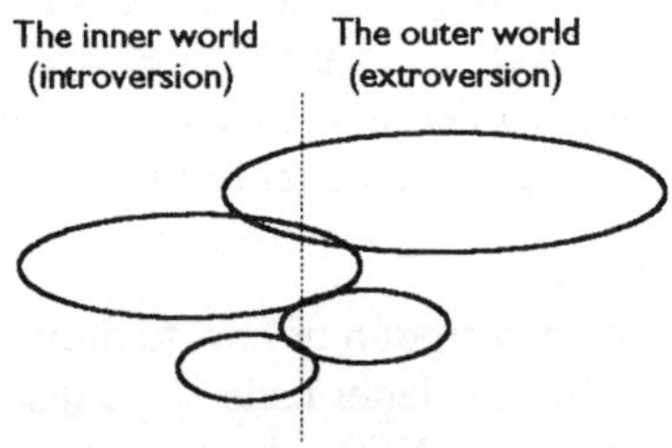

4. *Write the name of the function that is used primarily in the outer world in the ellipse at the top of right hand side (the extroversion column). P points to the second letter, whilst J points to the third letter of the Myers Briggs type.* In the case of the ENFP, P points to N, so iNtuition can be written at the top of the right hand column.

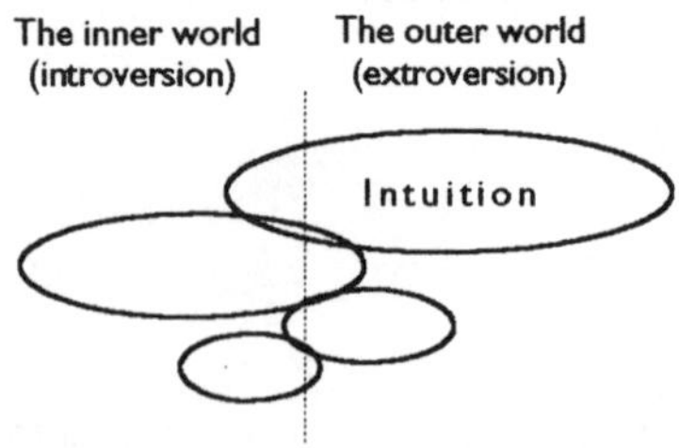

5. *Write the name of the other preferred function in the top ellipse*

of the other column. In the case of the ENFP, Feeling is written in the top of the Introversion column.

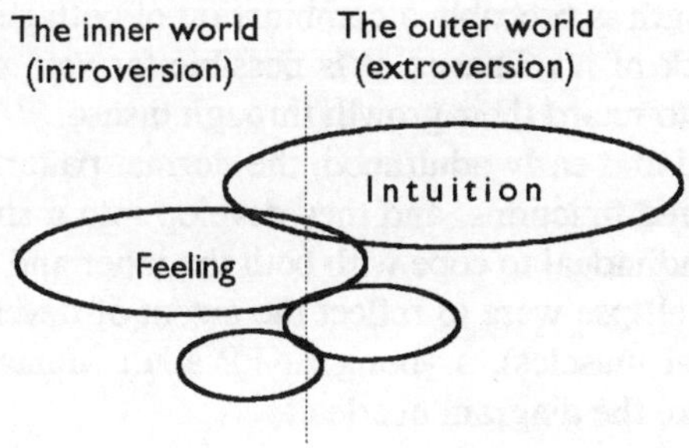

6. *Write the preference opposite to the dominant in the bottom ellipse, then write in the name of the remaining function.* For the ENFP, Sensing is opposite of iNtuition, so it is the Inferior function.

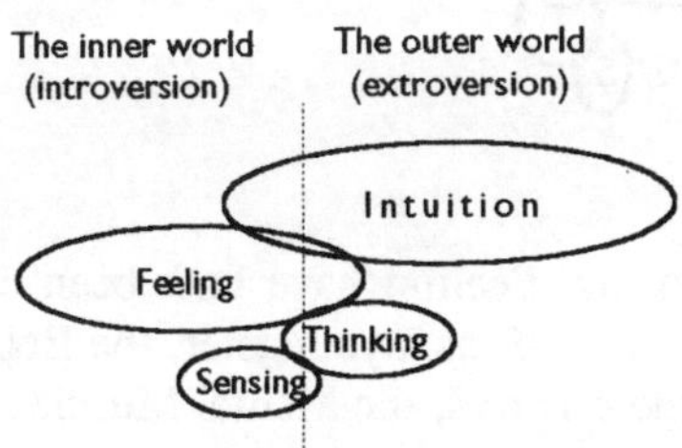

Activity 38 *Draw the diagram for an ISTJ. Check your answer with the appropriate chapter later in this book.*

If you produced the wrong result, reread the previous few pages that describe the steps involved, and keep the solution for ISTJ in front of you. Try to draw the diagram for other Myers Briggs types as well.

Mental muscles

Each of the functions - Sensing, iNtuition, Thinking and Feeling - are themselves dynamic. That is, they grow and develop with use, which is similar to the way that physical muscles grow. In fact, it can be useful to think of them as mental muscles, and the diagram you have just drawn is called a Mental Muscle Diagram.

The size of your mental muscles is not limitless but, as with normal muscles, their strength is probably a combination of both genetic make up and exercise, or lack of it. That is, it is possible for you to develop your mental muscles, or to retard their growth through disuse.

During childhood and early adulthood, the normal pattern of behaviour is to use our preferred functions, and they develop into a strong combination to enable the individual to cope with both the inner and outer worlds.

If the size of the ellipse were to reflect the extent of development of the functions (or mental muscles), a young ENFP adult Mental Muscle Diagram might look like the diagram overleaf:

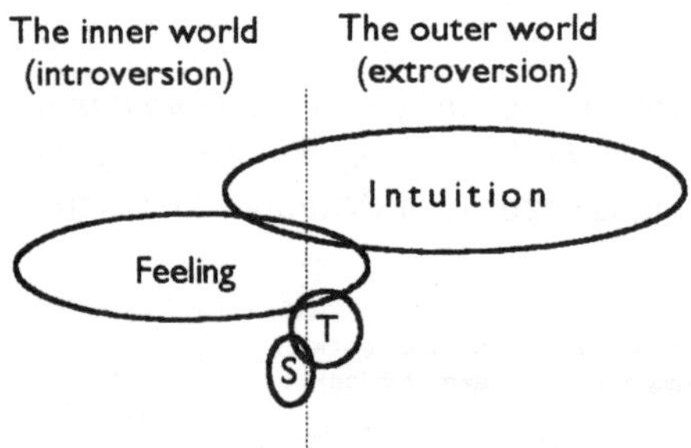

In this instance, iNtuition and Feeling have both been developed, and Thinking and Sensing have not. If, as a youngster, the ENFP had undergone extensive training in the sciences, the Mental Muscle diagram might look like this:

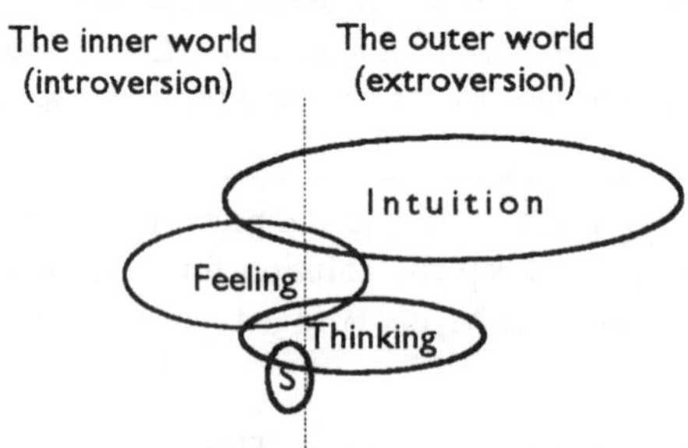

This may seem to have a better balance than the previous model. However, note that Feeling is somewhat smaller, and Thinking somewhat bigger than in the previous version of the diagram. Could it be that the Feeling preference has been underdeveloped? Is there any stress that results from overuse of the Thinking function? Does the individual have difficulty in deciding, because of the roughly equal sizes of the Thinking and Feeling functions. If they are equal, they may waste energy in competing, as logical considerations are of an equal and opposite force to personal values. Could some dyslexia-type problems result from a lack of differentiation between the Feeling and Thinking preference?

These questions provide a glimpse of how Myers Briggs can be used, amongst other things, in a personal counselling context. Developing adequate differentiation of the functions can help the individual to adapt more readily to various situations in life, and to reduce stress.

Activity 39 *Draw your own Mental Muscle diagram, showing the split between the outer and inner worlds. Make the size of each ellipse correspond with how often you use it by comparison with the other functions. Does the diagram show any difference between how you view yourself, and how others view you?*

You can check that the basics of the diagram are right by comparing your diagram with the one listed in the appropriate chapter later in this book.

When looking at the differences between how you see yourself and how others see you, compare the extroverted functions (which is what others mostly see) with the introverted functions (which is what you mostly see of yourself).

Being aware of the dynamic view of Myers Briggs, and the difference between what you see and what is inside, can help greatly in recognising type.

The shadow

A special note needs to be made about 'the shadow', which is a hidden aspect of our behaviour. We all have a part of ourselves that we do not like to admit, and therefore put it out of our conscious minds. It is often visible to others, whilst we cannot see it in ourselves - that is, it is subconscious. Sometimes, we 'project' it onto others - that is, we see it in other people, whilst denying its presence in ourselves.

The shadow is 'out of character' behaviour that can appear at any time, either fleetingly or for long periods of time. The circumstances when it is most likely to appear include being ill, under severe stress, or fatigued. It can also appear when you are forced to use the least preferred function for any significant time.

The shadow is a negative form of the type opposite to your Myers Briggs type. For example, the shadow of an ENFP is ISTJ. Under mild stress, the ENFP acts more and more like an ENFP, but there comes a point when the stress becomes too much, and the shadow appears - a negative form of ISTJ. The ENFP shadow is therefore preoccupied with irrelevant and meaningless detail, and critical of others.

Shadow behaviour is a part of a normal personality. When the shadow appears, it can be an indicator of stress, illness, fatigue, or simply that the individual has had to do a lot of work using the tertiary or inferior function.

When trying to recognise type in others, it is important to realise that you can sometimes be observing the shadow. It can usually be recognised by its negative form, and may be accompanied by apparent stress, ill-temper, or other negative characteristics. To find out more about the shadow, read 'Navigating Mid-life' or 'Beside Ourselves', details of which are given in the Appendix.

Type tables

There is one more technique that may help you to recognise type. In Appendix 2, there is a table, with a box for each of the 16 Myers Briggs types. In each box there is space for you to write the names of a few people that you recognise as being of that type.

Over the next few days and weeks, fill in this table with the names of people you know, as and when you work out what type they are. This will enable you to build a degree of familiarity with each personality type. By including a few names in each box, you will also gain a better understanding of both the common themes and the variations that can occur within any one particular type.

Conclusion

Recognising type is a task that requires skill, practice and a good understanding of the Myers Briggs model. Where preferences are not immediately obvious, the dynamic view of a person can be particularly useful in helping to gain insight and understanding. Classic temperament can also help, and it is always useful to be aware of the complications of learned behaviour, and the shadow.

Activity 40 *What Myers Briggs type is Sherlock Holmes?*

There is evidence to support the presence of most of the preferences in Sherlock Holmes' behaviour.

At times Sherlock Holmes appears to enjoy solitude, becoming wrapped up in his own thoughts. He does not have a large circle of friends, and seems to become an expert in his chosen fields - taking his knowledge to a degree of depth unmatched by his peers. On the other hand, he is energised by events in the world, which spur him to action: 'The game is afoot, Watson'. He revels in the theatrical, and is stimulated by the continual feud with his arch enemy - Professor Moriarty - and the vying debate with his brother.

There is strong evidence to support both Sensing and iNtuition as being his preferred means of perceiving. He is excellent at both observing detail and perceiving hidden meanings and seeing patterns in that detail.

He is clearly a logical person, and understanding how others feel is not a strong point. This implies a clear preference for Thinking.

There is evidence to support both J and P as a lifestyle. On the one hand, he is able to be flexible and pursue whichever line of reasoning seems appropriate. Also, he does not decide too quickly, and this would imply a Perceptive lifestyle. However, he is also determined to reach a conclusion, and the few failures that he has send him into a deep depression, when he often resorts to drug taking.

The only clear preference, at first glance, seems to be T.

Consider, now, the dynamic model. T is a clear preference, F is clearly weak, and S and N are closely balanced. This implies that T is dominant, F is the inferior, and S and N form the middle two functions. So the mental muscle diagram can be drawn with the T at the top, and F at the bottom.

However, we need to know whether the Thinking function is extroverted or introverted. The answer is in the clarity of his logic. If it was introverted, the Thinking function would not be too clear. As it is very apparent to all, this implies that the function is extroverted. So the diagram, so far, looks like:

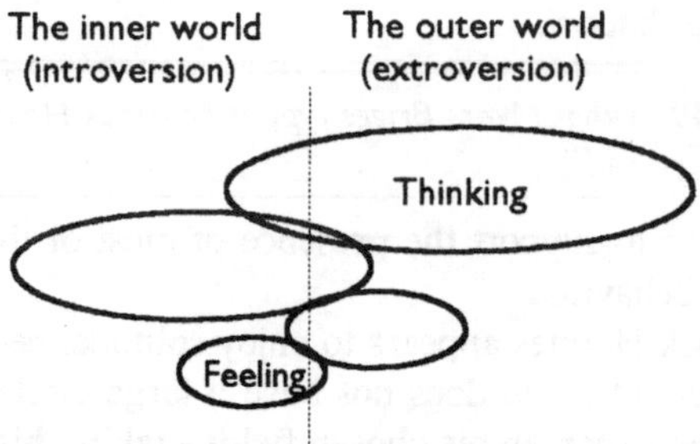

This is either ESTJ or ENTJ - but which? At this point it is useful to refer to the classic temperament. ESTJ is driven by a need to be of service, and fulfil duty. There is certainly some of this about Sherlock Holmes. However, he is very selective about who he 'provides service' to, choosing only those problems to solve which will provide him with sufficient challenge. ENTJ is driven by a search for competence, quality or excellence which, in my view, seems to fit a little better than ESTJ. Holmes strives to be expert in any field to which he turns. The final mental muscle diagram is therefore:

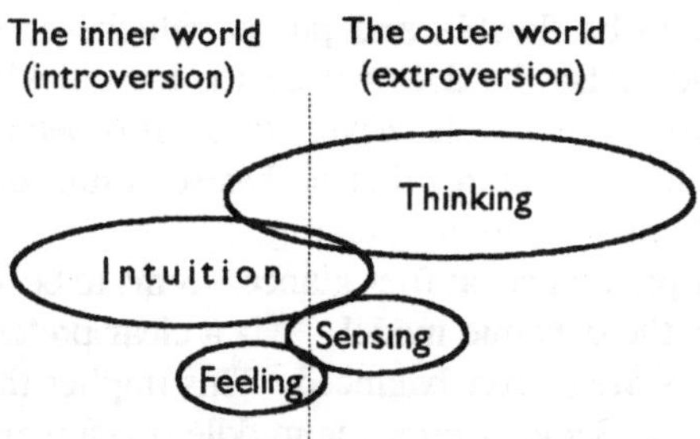

This diagram explains some aspects of Sherlock Holmes' character.

- His logical analysis is dominant, and evident to all
- His attention to detail is also evident because, although it is not the preferred mode of perception, it is extroverted. When perceiving data, Sherlock Holmes is therefore likely to say or do something that draws attention to that data, rather than share his insight. This is, in fact, what he does ('Look, Watson, a cigar of

Peruvian origin...')

- His iNtuition is introverted. Whilst he perceives patterns in the data, he is likely to retain that insight within his inner world of contemplation. This is very consistent with his behaviour, as he rarely spontaneously explains his insights, keeping Watson in the dark about his 'hunches', and simply pointing to how illogical the facts are.
- His shadow is ISFP, which in a negative form tends to withdraw, act impulsively, and can have negative feelings towards himself or others that may not be expressed. This is consistent with his introvert behaviour, which is often accompanied by drug taking, and a lack of tolerance of Dr Watson. This would suggest that much of what is seen as his introvert side is actually the Shadow.
- His disorganised, messy personality also appears mostly during his times of introversion, with all the negative characteristics that could be associated with the shadow.

It seems that Sherlock Holmes was an extrovert who led a life more in keeping with an introvert. If he were to want advice on how to reduce stress, one action he could consider might be to recognise and nurture his extrovert needs. However, there may be experiences in his past that have discouraged him from much contact with the outer world, resulting in his spending so much time in his shadow.

The Sherlock Holmes stories were written some 20 - 30 years before Jung produced his theories of psychological type, upon which Myers Briggs is based. It is a tribute to the excellent characterisation by Sir Arthur Conan Doyle that his fictional creation should so clearly conform to a modern understanding of personality.

Activity 41 *What Myers Briggs type is Ebeneezer Scrooge? In what part of the story do you see his shadow operating?*

There is no answer for this one - just a topic for you to debate with your friends.

6 Working with the 16 Myers Briggs types

Most of the remainder of this book contains detailed descriptions of the 16 Myers Briggs types. You will find the following notes useful preparation for reading these chapters.

A special note about Introverts

Each chapter contains a brief description of the dominant function, its orientation (whether it is introverted or extroverted), what difference that orientation makes, and what influence the auxiliary has on the dominant. It is particularly useful to remember the nature of the dominant when dealing with Introverts. The dominant is largely hidden to the casual observer, who can therefore misunderstand the personality of the Introvert.

Activity 42 *Draw the Mental Muscle Diagram for an INTJ. What is the casual observer likely to see? What is most important to the INTJ?*

From the diagram you should be able to tell that the casual observer is likely to see the extroverted logic. Logical decision-making may appear to be the most important aspect of the INTJ's character. However, it is the introverted iNtuition that is dominant, which can explain occasional uncharacteristic lack of logic in the INTJ's arguments.

An INTJ may have a clear vision of what he wants to achieve, and use strong logical argument in support of that vision. However, if it becomes apparent that the logical argument produces a result that is in conflict with his iNtuition, he may quickly change the basis of his argument. To the observer, a highly logical person has just made a totally irrational step.

However, if the observer makes the effort to understand the individual's vision, or iNtuitive understanding, the change in argument can be understood. Sometimes it can be difficult to get the INTJ to articulate his inner thoughts, so you need to patiently use open questions in order to find them out, bearing in mind that

- the INTJ expresses his/her vision or understanding in terms of logical options - to use the analogy of a novel: the sub-text is expressed, but the main plot remains hidden
- the casual observer believes the logical argument is paramount, and tries to engage the extroverted Thinking in discussion
- the INTJ may tend to criticise others' arguments, rather than articulate his own vision (i.e. use Thinking in the outer world of actions and spoken words)

So the introvert can be hard to read, as the casual observer is more likely to see the auxiliary function, rather then the dominant function that remains hidden, visible only in subtle ways. When dealing with introverts, therefore, be constantly mindful of the dominant function within, and avoid the trap of engaging discussion just with that part of the personality that is extroverted.

Classic temperament

The four classic temperaments are described excellently in Kiersey & Bates' book (1978), details of which are given in the Appendix. The four temperaments differ in basic motivation and drive.

- The Apollonian or Choleric temperament (-NF- types) is driven by a search for meaning or purpose.
- The Promethean or Phlegmatic temperament (-NT- types) is driven by a search for competence, quality or excellence.
- The Dionesian or Sanguine temperament (-S-P types) is driven by a desire to be free from constraint, to experience and enjoy life.
- The Epimethean or Melancholic temperament (-S-J types) is driven by a need to belong, be of service and fulfil duty.

Awareness of the temperament of colleagues with whom you work can be very useful in making your working relationships more productive. The manager of a team, in particular, can allocate work and responsibilities to play to the strengths of each team member, rather than working against them. For example:

- Give NF's responsibility for work that has meaning and purpose.

Explain why it is being done, and who will benefit.

- Give NTs a challenge, that allows them to increase their own competence, or improve quality.
- Give SPs freedom to operate within their own guideline. Agree the boundaries within which the SP must work, but then let him get on with it without continually looking over his shoulder.
- Make SJs feel included in what is going on. Involve them in relevant meetings, and recognise their steadfast and faithful hard work.

It is important to remember that each person is an individual. The detailed descriptions in this book should not be regarded as a magic formula that will work wonders, but as a tool kit of ideas, some of which will work better than others, depending on the individual. It can be most useful when used as the basis for discussion between colleagues, or a manager and subordinate, to recognise your respective styles, and identify how the working relationship can be structured for the benefit of both.

7 ENTP

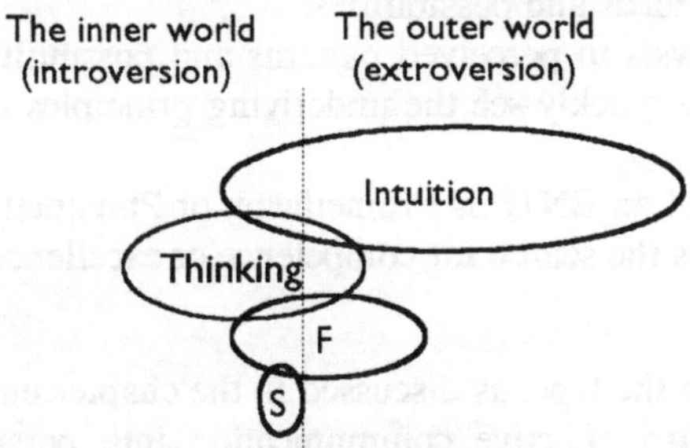

What makes an ENTP tick?

The Dominant function is the perceptive one of iNtuition. Characteristics associated with this function include:

- Likes looking at information from a global viewpoint, spotting patterns and relationships, that lead to an understanding of the key issues
- Focuses more on possibilities for the future than the here-and-now
- Enjoys change, challenge, and variety

The perceptive iNtuition function is extroverted. That is, iNtuition is used primarily to govern the outer world of actions and spoken words. The ENTP will therefore:

- Try ideas out, to explore new possibilities and discover, by experience, which ones work
- Change procedures to see if any improvement can be made, rather than just operate them
- Be interested primarily in evolutionary development, perhaps

with an eye on the strategy.
- Be more interested in exploring ideas than bringing them to closure

The iNtuition function is primarily supported by introverted Thinking judgement. That is, Thinking judgement is used primarily to manage the inner world of thoughts and emotions. This will modify the way that the iNtuition is directed, by:

- focusing the (outer world) iNtuition on ideas and possibilities that relate to systems and concepts
- inwardly tending to spot the flaws in situations, people or ideas. Rather than expressing criticism directly, it may surface in the form of contradictory ideas and possibilities.
- applying logical analysis to perceived patterns and possibilities, enabling the ENTP to quickly see the underlying principles in a situation

The classic temperament of an ENTP is Promethean, or Phlegmatic, for whom a basic driving force is the search for competence or excellence.

Persuading an ENTP

Take a style appropriate to the type, as discussed in the chapter on basic interpersonal skills. To turn effective communication into persuasive communication, you should also consider the following points:

- The main currency of communication should be principles, competence and the strive for excellence or quality
- Discuss the theoretical aspects of your proposal, and any research undertaken, to open up discussion on the principles involved
- Let the ENTP discover the key principles or issues that underlie your proposal
- If the criteria that the ENTP is using to evaluate ideas are not clear (Thinking is introverted) and you need to know, then ask open questions to find out what they are.
- Discuss a broad range of possibilities for the future, and show how your proposal can help achieve the ENTP's vision or support his/her strategy
- Ensure the presentation is presented competently, all assertions are credible, and show how your proposal will increase quality

You should concentrate on appealing to the ENTP's dominant function - extroverted iNtuition. That is, support the ENTP's capacity for exploring ideas and desire to learn.

Motivating an ENTP

An ENTP will find tasks enjoyable or motivating if they involve:

- innovation and creativity, particularly in conceptual discussions about systems, strategies and models
- enabling the organisation to grow and develop
- tackling challenging and complex problems, particularly those that require the development of strategy
- debating issues in groups
- breaking new ground
- high level objectives, where the style of delivery is in the hands of the ENTP
- responding to increasing demands for quality and excellence

An ENTP will find tasks uncomfortable or demotivating if they involve:

- doing someone else's work
- routine paperwork or administrative details
- having to follow a strict agenda, particularly if someone else has set it
- operating procedures where there is no requirement for change or improvement
- being closely supervised
- working in isolation

Leading an ENTP

An ENTP will particularly appreciate a leader who:

- gives the ENTP autonomy to achieve challenging objectives
- is competent, respects the competence of the ENTP, and will debate the issues underlying his/her ideas
- focuses on global outcomes, rather than the detail of implementation
- gives the ENTP a broad portfolio, with the ability to extend it further
- gives the ENTP freedom to innovate

Contributions to the team of an ENTP

In a team environment, the ENTP can contribute by:

- challenging the status quo, and encouraging other team members to achieve more than they thought they could
- leading other team members to a greater understanding of the concepts and principles involved
- involving people who are competent in relevant skills

- contributing creative ideas on how the task can be achieved or quality improved
- creating new ideas out of confrontational discussion
- finding ways to overcome apparently insurmountable difficulties
- generating team spirit though the ENTP's own energy and enthusiasm

The potential ways in which an ENTP can irritate others include:

- initiating too many projects, and not being able to deliver on all of them
- introducing too much change, and not leaving well-established, workable routines alone
- not taking sufficient account of current realities
- appearing competitive and unappreciative of the contribution of others
- leaving someone else to do the routine work
- making errors of fact

As with all types, the ENTP can achieve personal growth by developing all functions that are not fully developed, through actions such as:

- being selective about the initiation of projects
- pausing and thinking, and recognising that others will accept the ENTP and his/her ideas more if their own contributions are accepted and valued
- appreciating the value of existing routines that work well
- investigating the facts, and documenting them, before interpreting what they mean
- taking time to consider the impact of the ENTP's approach and ideas on people's feelings
- expressing appreciation towards others

Recognising Stress

As stress increases, 'learned behaviour' tends to give way to the natural style, so the ENTP will behave more according to type when under greater stress. For example, in a crisis, the ENTP might:

- spend time brainstorming ideas, and debating or critiquing what needs to be done
- provide a lot of drive, but try to do too much
- draft in people with proven skills to work on the problem
- make errors of fact, or ignore routine matters that might nevertheless be essential

Under extreme stress, fatigue or illness, the ENTP's shadow may appear - a negative form of ISFJ. Example characteristics are:

- being pedantic about unimportant details
- doing things to excess - e.g.: eating, drinking or exercising
- expressing emotions in an intensive and uncontrolled way
- being very sensitive to criticism

The shadow is part of the unconscious that is often visible to others, onto whom the shadow is projected. The ENTP may therefore readily see these faults in others without recognising it in him/her self.

Stress Management

Ways of reducing stress include:

- to recognise and distinguish between one's true preference and learned behaviour, due to cultural, parental or employment demands.
- to structure one's life to allow more use of true preferences

Some ideas for reducing the ENTP's stress in the workplace are:

- learning to value the contribution that an ENTP can make in the work situation
- educating colleagues so that they also value the contribution of the ENTP's true preference
- finding a role that allows the ENTP to increase his/her own competence and achieve new levels of excellence
- having high level objectives to achieve, with a flexible agenda. This provides the freedom to achieve the goals in the ENTP's own way, probably with periodic intensive bursts of energy rather than steady progression towards the goal
- having a good secretary or assistant (with dominant Sensing) who will look after the paperwork, administer the routine jobs, and advise on the practicality of the ENTP's ideas
- seeking to work more in groups than alone
- having an open plan office, with somewhere to retire for privacy, when needed
- allowing plenty of opportunity for intellectual debate
- undertaking a programme of learning to increase the ENTP's skills and competence

8 ISFJ

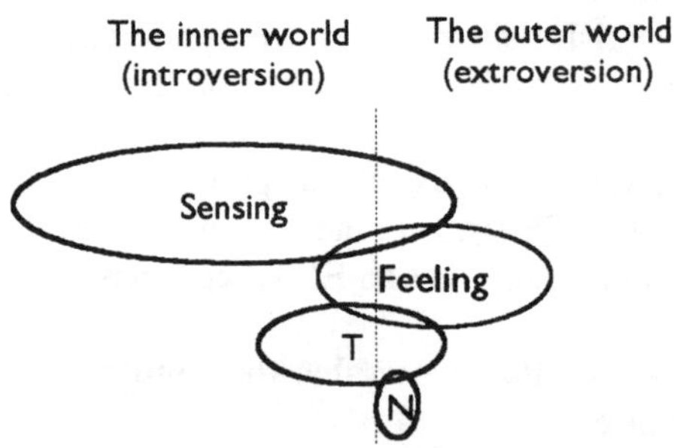

What makes an ISFJ tick?

The Dominant function is the perceptive one of Sensing. Characteristics associated with this function include:

- Likes looking at information in terms of facts and details
- Focuses more on the here and now rather than possibilities for the future
- Feels comfortable in areas of proven experience
- Takes a realistic approach

The perceptive Sensing function is introverted. That is, Sensing is used primarily to govern the inner world of thoughts and emotions. The ISFJ will therefore:

- Seek to develop a realistic understanding of the world as it is, in the light of what he/she observes
- Be pragmatic in nature, constantly learning to adapt to the world as it is now
- Observe in a subjective way, selecting and relating facts that others would not, and seeing those facts more in terms of

impressions and significance than pure fact

The Sensing function is primarily supported by extroverted Feeling judgement, That is, Feeling judgement is used primarily to manage the outer world of actions and spoken words. This will modify the way that the Sensing is directed, by:

- focusing the (inner world) Sensing on ideas and possibilities that relate to people
- expressing appreciation for the contributions of others, particularly where they have done or said something that the ISFJ sees as significant
- making decisions on the basis of values that support the ISFJ's understanding of the world
- reinforcing the subjectivity of observation

The classic temperament of an ISFJ is Epimethean, or Melancholic, for whom a basic driving force is duty, service and the need to belong.

Persuading an ISFJ

Take a style appropriate to the type, as discussed in the chapter on basic interpersonal skills. To turn effective communication into persuasive communication, you should also consider the following points:

- The main currency of communication should be relationships, harmony and service
- Discuss the practical results for people, especially where it helps the ISFJ and those he/she cares about.
- Use case studies, ideally with personal references, to illustrate who has benefited to date, and state the benefits explicitly
- Discuss the positive impact on relationships, building harmony, and ensuring everyone's talents are used
- Set your proposal in a personal context and show it provides immediate benefits
- Avoid conflict during your presentation
- Let the ISFJ determine what is significant in your presentation - the ISFJ may not express such views - so ask

You should concentrate on appealing to the ISFJ's dominant function - introverted Sensing. That is, support the ISFJ's understanding of the world, and build on those facts the ISFJ sees as significant. It is possible to misunderstand the ISFJ, and believe that the extroverted Feeling is paramount (i.e.: certain values are of overriding importance). However, the inward focus on practical objectives, and perception of the world, is more important. Feeling judgement is used in support of this. The ISFJ may therefore:

- appear to drop values once held as vital, if they start to result in the ISFJ's objectives and enjoyment of the world being frustrated rather than helped
- appear to go along with a proposition put to the ISFJ, but then ignore it in practice - an ISFJ sometimes finds conflict or criticism difficult (both giving and receiving it)

It is therefore important to encourage the ISFJ to share introverted Sensing thoughts, so that you can find out what his (subjective) understanding of the situation is. You may not be able to dissuade the ISFJ from that subjective impression, and may have to work with it rather than against it. As with all introverts, don't assume that silence means agreement.

Motivating an ISFJ

An ISFJ will find tasks enjoyable or motivating if they involve:

- helping people and seeing them derive pleasure from the service
- applying experience to practical work
- giving and receiving appreciation
- compiling information about people
- the ability to achieve goals as a result of hard conscientious work
- building relationships and reducing conflict
- working with individuals, particularly in a fun (but not superficial) way
- a structured working environment, over which the ISFJ can exert control

An ISFJ will find tasks uncomfortable or demotivating if they involve:

- experimenting with something new
- conceptual discussions and analysis
- criticising others, especially in a group or with people the ISFJ knows well
- receiving criticism
- working with costs, and figures rather than people
- a high degree of ambiguity about objectives, responsibilities etc.
- playing politics or using conflict as a tool to increase performance
- working with large groups
- having to work in an unpredictable environment, over which the ISFJ has little control, and to which he/she has to respond

spontaneously
- establishing hierarchies, divisions of status, or other potential barriers between people

Leading an ISFJ

An ISFJ will particularly appreciate a leader who:

- sets clear goals and deadlines that can be achieved using established procedures
- establishes a structured environment with little ambiguity
- is sociable and friendly
- sets a personal example, that the ISFJ can follow, of being well organised and working hard
- has a clear sense of personal responsibility, adhering to clear personal values of integrity, respect, punctuality, consideration, etc.
- puts a high priority on communication, and the involvement of people in decision making
- uses a positive and personal approach - praising, encouraging and building rapport

Contributions to the team of an ISFJ

In a team environment, the ISFJ can contribute by:

- working hard and efficiently to complete tasks by the deadlines set
- building team spirit through maintaining good relationships with each team member, being accepting of their contributions, and promoting harmony and co-operation
- contributing practical skills in organising people
- ensuring that everyone in the team feels valued, and that their needs are met
- asking for contributions from all team members, and seeking to arrive at consensus decisions
- maintaining respect for established hierarchies and traditions
- striving to ensure that people are happy with the service provided

The potential ways in which an ISFJ can irritate others include:

- avoiding conflict, and not giving criticism when it is needed
- not articulating his/her understanding of the situation
- not seeing the wood for the trees
- failing to state his/her own needs
- being too serious
- not promoting his/her own ideas or achievements

As with all types, the ISFJ can achieve personal growth by developing all functions that are not fully developed, through actions such as:

- articulating more of the ISFJ's own views
- developing a long term vision, that avoids focusing on details
- assertiveness training
- being more forthright, and offering direct criticism
- learning to promote the ISFJ's ideas and achievements to others, recognising that others may well find them valuable
- undertaking a formal process of evaluation against criteria, including a cost benefit analysis

Recognising Stress

As stress increases, 'learned behaviour' tends to give way to the natural style, so the ISFJ will behave more according to type when under greater stress. For example, in a crisis, the ISFJ might:

- find a place of solitude in which to think and work
- value the efforts of others and appreciate their encouragement
- use tried and trusted means of solving problems, possibly failing to recognise the need for change
- use pragmatic solutions at the expense of the long term

Under extreme stress, fatigue or illness, the ISFJ's shadow may appear - a negative form of ENTP. Example characteristics are:

- being very intolerant of others who do not act competently
- suggesting impractical ideas
- being critical of others, and finding fault with almost everything
- having a gloomy view of the future
- being argumentative

The shadow is part of the unconscious that is often visible to others, onto whom the shadow is projected. The ISFJ may therefore readily see these faults in others without recognising it in him/her self.

Stress Management

Ways of reducing stress include:

- to recognise and distinguish between one's true preference and learned behaviour, due to cultural, parental or employment demands.
- to structure one's life to allow more use of true preferences

Some ideas for reducing the ISFJ's stress in the workplace are:

- learning to value the contribution that an ISFJ can make in the work situation

- educating colleagues so that they also value the contribution of the ISFJ's true preference
- finding a practical role that enables the ISFJ to be of service to people
- having a private office or quiet area to work, with access to people when interaction is needed
- having clear objectives to achieve
- dealing with people on a one-to-one basis

9 INFP

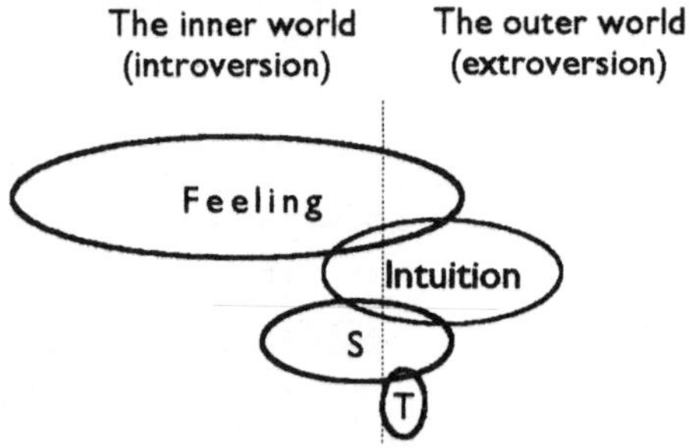

What makes an INFP tick?

The Dominant function is the judging one of Feeling. Characteristics associated with this function include:

- Makes decisions on the basis of personal values
- Is appreciative and accepting of people - enjoying company and seeking harmony
- Assesses the impact of decisions on others, being sympathetic or compassionate
- Takes a personal approach

The judging Feeling function is introverted. That is, Feeling is used primarily to govern the inner world of thoughts and emotions. The INFP will therefore:

- develop an inner emotional life that is often unseen to others, but is experienced as intense
- retain a strong sense of values, which are often not expressed
- emotionally accept or reject various aspects of life - for example, deciding whether praise or criticism received is valid and, at

extreme, ignoring whatever is unacceptable

- feel appreciation towards others, but not express it

The Feeling function is primarily supported by extroverted iNtuitive perception, That is, iNtuitive perception is used primarily to manage the outer world of actions and spoken words. This will modify the way that the Feeling is directed, by:

- focusing the (inner world) Feeling on ideas and possibilities for people
- looking for meaningful relationships
- deciding on friendships through insight into their personality and motivation

The classic temperament of an INFP is Apollonian, or Choleric, for whom a basic driving force is the search for meaning or purpose.

Persuading an INFP

Take a style appropriate to the type, as discussed in the chapter on basic interpersonal skills. To turn effective communication into persuasive communication, you should also consider the following points:

- The main currency of communication should be people's value, abilities and contributions
- Discuss the positive impact on people, especially where it facilitates insight, growth and development.
- Include a substantial element of (purposeful) fun in your proposal so that participants will enjoy it.
- Discuss the positive impact on relationships, building harmony, and ensuring everyone's talents are used
- Let the INFP discover how your proposal relates to his/her personal values, and therefore has meaning or purpose
- Avoid conflict during your presentation
- The INFP may come to conclusions that are not expressed - so ask.

You should concentrate on appealing to the INFP's dominant function - introverted Feeling. That is, support the INFP's deeply held values. It is possible to misunderstand the INFP, and believe that the extroverted iNtuition is paramount (e.g.: he has an important vision towards which he is working, or he is driven by a desire to learn and understand). However, there are some core values that are paramount and may not be articulated that take precedence over the extroverted iNtuition. The INFP may therefore appear to be adaptable, flexible and inquisitive until the point when his inner values are violated. At this point, the INFP would dig his heels in and surprise everyone at the strength of his stance.

It is therefore important to:

- encourage the INFP to share introverted Feeling thoughts, so that you can find out what his values are
- not assume that the lack of disagreement implies agreement, as the introverted feeling is both reticent to speak, and wary of conflict.

Motivating an INFP

An INFP will find tasks enjoyable or motivating if they involve:

- innovation and creativity
- facilitating individuals' growth through insight
- improving team productivity through realising the potential of the individual team members
- building relationships and reducing conflict
- working with groups, in an atmosphere of openness and trust
- breaking new ground
- receiving appreciation

An INFP will find tasks uncomfortable or demotivating if they involve:

- routine paperwork
- playing politics or using conflict as a tool to increase performance
- working with costs and figures rather than people
- producing and administering implementation plans
- a practical, hard-headed approach
- providing a service purely to satisfy others

Leading an INFP

An INFP will particularly appreciate a leader who:

- builds an environment of friendliness and trust
- establishes an inspiring vision - one with meaning or purpose that the INFP can believe in
- acknowledges the INFP's uniqueness - allowing opportunity for personal growth
- allows the INFP privacy and space to think, and then listens well to his/her ideas
- demonstrates a caring for people
- offers praise and encouragement

Contributions to the team of an INFP

In a team environment, the INFP can contribute by:

- promoting insight and common understanding amongst the team
- contributing well thought out and innovative ideas
- generating team spirit though sensitive listening and a quiet enthusiasm
- focusing on areas of agreement and building on others' proposals
- where there are areas of disagreement, exploring a wide range of options to see if a point of agreement can be found

The potential ways in which an INFP can irritate others include:

- being idealistic
- appearing out of touch, perhaps not fully recognising current realities, and disregarding those they find unacceptable
- being stubborn over issues the group did not anticipate being a problem
- spending too much time thinking
- avoiding conflict and not giving forthright criticism when it is needed
- focusing so much on interpersonal issues that cost and other impersonal considerations are not adequately discussed

As with all types, the INFP can achieve personal growth by developing all functions that are not fully developed, through actions such as:

- being prepared to declare the INFP's personal values
- investigating and recognising the facts before interpreting what they mean
- listing options and undertaking a formal process of evaluation against criteria, including a cost benefit analysis
- undertaking a critical appraisal of a situation or person, and expressing disagreement or criticism when it could be of value to the recipient
- focusing on impersonal details during discussions and when making decisions
- listing options and undertaking a formal process of evaluation against criteria, including a cost benefit analysis
- establishing a long term goal, preparing a detailed implementation plan, and sticking to it

Recognising Stress

As stress increases, 'learned behaviour' tends to give way to the natural style, so the INFP will behave more according to type when under greater stress. For example, in a crisis, the INFP might:

- concentrate only on what the INFP sees as important
- work alone if possible
- contribute creative ideas, but overlook current realities
- fail to consider the cost implications

Under extreme stress, fatigue or illness, the INFP's shadow may appear - a negative form of ESTJ. Example characteristics are:

- being very critical and find fault with almost everything
- doing things to excess - e.g.: eating, drinking or exercising
- becoming bossy or domineering and ignoring others' feelings
- being pedantic about unimportant details

The shadow is part of the unconscious that is often visible to others, onto whom the shadow is projected. The INFP may therefore readily see these faults in others without recognising it in him/her self.

Stress Management

Ways of reducing stress include:

- to recognise and distinguish between one's true preference and learned behaviour, due to cultural, parental or employment demands.
- to structure one's life to allow more use of true preferences

Some ideas for reducing the INFP's stress in the workplace are:

- learning to value the contribution that an INFP can make in the work situation
- educating colleagues so that they also value the contribution of the INFP's preferences
- finding a role that has meaning or purpose, perhaps in the area of development of people, that does not involve politics or significant conflict
- having high level objectives to achieve, with a flexible agenda. This provides the freedom to achieve the goals in the INFP's own way.
- allowing plenty of opportunity for positive feedback from colleagues or clients
- having a good secretary or assistant who will look after the paperwork and administration
- having a private office, with the ability to meet people when needed

10 ESTP

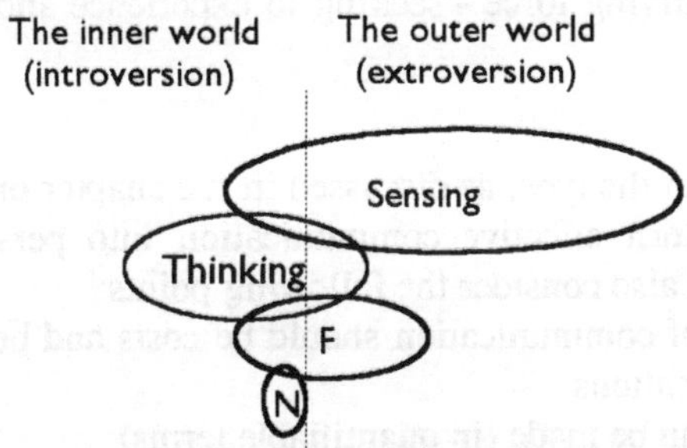

What makes an ESTP tick?

The Dominant function is the perceptive one of Sensing. Characteristics associated with this function include:

- Likes looking at information in terms of facts and details
- Focuses more on the here and now rather than possibilities for the future
- Feels comfortable in areas of proven experience
- Takes a realistic approach

The perceptive Sensing function is extroverted. That is, Sensing is used primarily to govern the outer world of actions and spoken words. The ESTP will therefore:

- Seek to experience and enjoy the world as it is
- Be very responsive to current events, with life tending to be a succession of events
- Be pragmatic in nature, constantly seeking to change the world to the way the ESTP wants it to be
- Observe in an objective way, valuing facts without necessarily

putting an interpretation upon them

The Sensing function is primarily supported by introverted Thinking judgement. That is, Thinking judgement is used primarily to manage the inner world of thoughts and emotions. This will modify the way that the Sensing is directed, by:

- focusing the (outer world) Sensing on impersonal facts and logical options
- tending to enjoy action and events for themselves rather than for the company of others
- leading to enjoyment of material possessions

The classic temperament of an ESTP is Dionesian, or Sanguine, for whom freedom is a basic driving force - seeking to experience and enjoy life.

Persuading an ESTP

Take a style appropriate to the type, as discussed in the chapter on basic interpersonal skills. To turn effective communication into persuasive communication, you should also consider the following points:

- The main currency of communication should be costs and benefits of practical applications
- Show how savings can be made (in quantifiable terms)
- Translate benefits in terms of how they affect the bottom-line
- Answer all questions directly, and include an appropriate level of detail
- Strike whilst the iron is hot - the ESTP can be impulsive, so the urgent requirement today may not be so urgent tomorrow.

You should concentrate on appealing to the ESTP's dominant function - extroverted Sensing. That is, help the ESTP to discover relevant facts and enjoy his/her experience of the world.

Motivating an ESTP

An ESTP will find tasks enjoyable or motivating if they involve:

- solving urgent problems using proven methods - i.e. fire fighting
- variety, freedom and independence
- a degree of risk
- working with groups
- a fun, action-oriented environment

An ESTP will find tasks uncomfortable or demotivating if they involve:

- no ability to achieve short term objectives - e.g.: only long term research and development of strategy

- the need to stick to pre-defined procedures
- a highly structured environment, using lots of formal meetings
- working primarily with 'soft' issues to do with people - e.g.: insight, growth,
- working alone
- being closely supervised

Leading an ESTP

An ESTP will particularly appreciate a leader who:

- sets clear goals and deadlines
- encourages and rewards the taking of risks
- is direct in communication
- gives the ESTP headroom to achieve objectives in his/her way
- is efficient, fair, and flexible
- gives praise where praise is due, and criticism where criticism is due

Contributions to the team of an ESTP

In a team environment, the ESTP can contribute by:

- making things happen, with an action-oriented approach
- building a lively 'can-do' atmosphere, which generates team spirit
- focusing on practical ideas
- applying a common sense approach to problem solving
- maintaining awareness of the factual information on which discussions are based
- taking charge in a crisis, and organising others

The potential ways in which an ESTP can irritate others include:

- acting too quickly, without appearing to think things through
- focusing too much on the current task at the expense of longer term or interpersonal issues
- not seeing the wood for the trees
- not taking account of the sensitivities of others
- turning to a new problem before the last one has been fully completed
- seeming materialistic
- generating crises as a way of getting things moving

As with all types, the ESTP can achieve personal growth by developing all functions that are not fully developed, through actions such as:

- developing a long term vision, that avoids focusing on details

- developing a greater understanding of how people feel
- stopping and thinking before acting
- ensuring that all aspects of a task have been completed before going on to the next one
- spending time to interpret facts - looking for subjective meaning, and for underlying patterns
- developing time management skills
- deciding on a personal set of values, and revisiting this list from time to time
- expressing appreciation to others for their qualities

Recognising Stress

As stress increases, 'learned behaviour' tends to give way to the natural style, so the ESTP will behave more according to type when under greater stress. For example, in a crisis, the ESTP might:

- use impulsive energy to overcome whatever obstacles get in the way
- generate new actions
- use tried and trusted means of solving problems
- use pragmatic solutions at the expense of the long term

Under extreme stress, fatigue or illness, the ESTP's shadow may appear - a negative form of INFJ. Example characteristics are:

- going quiet or withdrawing from people
- having a gloomy view of the future
- having intense negative feelings towards others, which may be openly expressed
- ceasing to adapt to changing circumstances

The shadow is part of the unconscious that is often visible to others, onto whom the shadow is projected. The ESTP may therefore readily see these faults in others without recognising it in him/her self.

Stress Management

Ways of reducing stress include:

- to recognise and distinguish between one's true preference and learned behaviour, due to cultural, parental or employment demands.
- to structure one's life to allow more use of true preferences

Some ideas for reducing the ESTP's stress in the workplace are:

- learning to value the contribution that an ESTP can make in the work situation

- educating colleagues so that they also value the contribution of the ESTP's true preference
- finding a practical role that involves responding to crises - e.g.: fire fighting, problem solving
- having an open plan office, with somewhere to retire for privacy when needed
- the job should be driven by external demands, rather than rely on the ESTP's inner resources to drive the work forward
- seeking to work more in groups than alone

11 ENFP

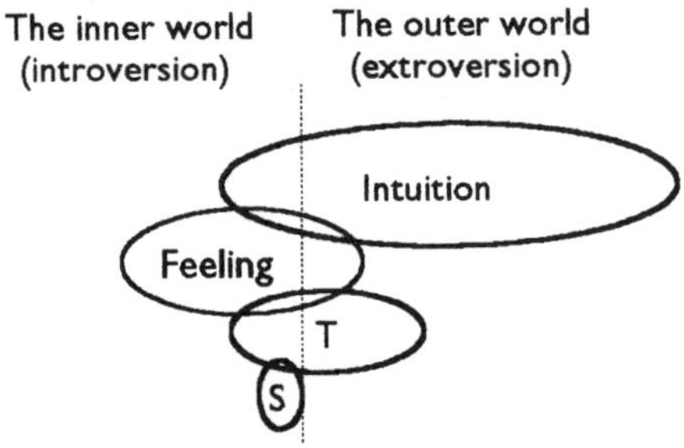

What makes an ENFP tick?

The Dominant function is the perceptive one of iNtuition. Characteristics associated with this function include:

- Likes looking at information from a global viewpoint, spotting patterns and relationships, that lead to an understanding of the key issues
- Focuses more on possibilities for the future than the here-and-now
- Enjoys change, challenge, and variety

The perceptive iNtuition function is extroverted. That is, iNtuition is used primarily to govern the outer world of actions and spoken words. The ENFP will therefore:

- Try ideas out, to explore new possibilities and discover, by experience, which ones work
- Change procedures to see if any improvement can be made, rather than just operate them
- Be interested in evolutionary development, but with an eye on the

strategy.

- Be more interested in exploring ideas than bringing them to closure

The iNtuition function is primarily supported by introverted Feeling judgement, That is, Feeling judgement is used primarily to manage the inner world of thoughts and emotions. This will modify the way that the iNtuition is directed, by:

- focusing the (outer world) iNtuition on ideas and possibilities that relate to people
- inwardly appreciating the contributions of others, though not expressing it that often.
- internally rejecting any options that clearly conflict with the ENFP's values - though the rejection might not be expressed or seen to others

The classic temperament of an ENFP is Apollonian, or Choleric, for whom a basic driving force is the search for meaning or purpose.

Persuading an ENFP

Take a style appropriate to the type, as discussed in the chapter on basic interpersonal skills. To turn effective communication into persuasive communication, you should also consider the following points:

- The main currency of communication should be people's value, abilities and contributions
- Discuss the positive impact on people, especially where it facilitates insight, growth and development.
- Include a substantial element of (purposeful) fun in your proposal so that participants will enjoy it.
- Discuss the positive impact on relationships, building harmony, and ensuring everyone's talents are used
- Let the ENFP discover how your proposal relates to his/her personal values, and therefore has meaning or purpose
- If the ENFP's values are not clear (Feeling is introverted) and you need to know, then ask open questions to find out what is really important to him/her. Such values may be difficult to discover if their expression might create conflict in the discussion.

You should concentrate on appealing to the ENFP's dominant function - extroverted iNtuition. That is, support the ENFP's vision, ideas, and enthusiasm.

Motivating an ENFP

An ENFP will find tasks enjoyable or motivating if they involve:

- innovation and creativity, particularly in changing people for the better
- giving people insight and allowing them to grow
- improving team productivity through a variety of ways
- building relationships and reducing conflict
- working with groups, particularly in a fun (but not superficial) way
- a flexible agenda, with freedom to explore
- receiving appreciation

An ENFP will find tasks uncomfortable or demotivating if they involve:

- routine paperwork
- playing politics or using conflict as a tool to increase performance
- working with costs, and figures rather than people
- working in isolation
- having to follow a strict agenda, particularly if someone else has set it
- establishing hierarchies, divisions of status, or other potential barriers between people
- receiving criticism

Leading an ENFP

An ENFP will particularly appreciate a leader who:

- builds an environment of friendliness and trust
- establishes an inspiring vision - one with meaning or purpose that the ENFP can believe in
- puts a high priority on communication, and the involvement of people in decision making
- uses a positive and personal approach - praising, encouraging and building rapport
- acknowledges the ENFP's uniqueness - allowing opportunity for personal growth
- gives the ENFP freedom to innovate and is open to his/her ideas

Contributions to the team of an ENFP

In a team environment, the ENFP can contribute by:

- acting as a catalyst for change, and encouraging the team to change together

- focusing on areas of agreement and building on others' proposals
- where there are areas of disagreement, exploring a wide range of options to see if a point of agreement can be found.
- contributing creative ideas, particularly those involving people
- including others in the process of developing ideas and vision, and being very accepting of contributions, even of varying quality
- generating team spirit though the ENFP's own energy and enthusiasm

The potential ways in which an ENFP can irritate others include:

- losing sight of the main purpose of the discussion and going off at tangents
- initiating too many projects, and not being able to deliver on all of them
- talking too much
- introducing too much change, and not leaving well-established, workable routines alone.
- making errors of fact
- wanting to pursue ideas without fully thinking through the consequences in, say, cost terms

As with all types, the ENFP can achieve personal growth by developing all functions that are not fully developed, through actions such as:

- being selective about starting projects, and producing plans to help identify which ones can be delivered
- pausing and thinking, and recognising that others will accept the ENFP and his/her ideas more if given sufficient time to make their own contribution
- being more accepting of existing routines that work well
- investigating the facts, and documenting them, before interpreting what they mean
- listing options and undertaking a formal process of evaluation against criteria, including a cost benefit analysis
- changing his/her vision to fit more closely with what is possible
- expressing the appreciation that is felt towards others

Recognising Stress

As stress increases, 'learned behaviour' tends to give way to the natural style, so the ENFP will behave more according to type when under greater stress. For example, in a crisis, the ENFP might:

- involve people in brainstorming ideas
- be democratic about choosing the solution to use
- provide a lot of drive, but try to do too much
- make errors of fact, or ignore routine matters that might nevertheless be essential

Under extreme stress, fatigue or illness, the ENFP's shadow may appear - a negative form of ISTJ. Example characteristics are:

- being pedantic about unimportant details
- doing things to excess - e.g.: eating, drinking or exercising
- being critical of others, and finding fault with almost everything
- taking charge without consideration to others

The shadow is part of the unconscious that is often visible to others, onto whom the shadow is projected. The ENFP may therefore readily see these faults in others without recognising it in him/her self.

Stress Management

Ways of reducing stress include:

- to recognise and distinguish between one's true preference and learned behaviour, due to cultural, parental or employment demands.
- to structure one's life to allow more use of true preferences

Some ideas for reducing the ENFP's stress in the workplace are:

- learning to value the contribution that an ENFP can make in the work situation
- educating colleagues so that they also value the contribution of the ENFP's true preference
- finding a role that has meaning or purpose, perhaps in the area of development of people, that does not involve politics or significant conflict
- having high level objectives to achieve, with a flexible agenda. This provides the freedom to achieve the goals in the ENFP's own way, probably with periodic intensive bursts of energy rather than steady progression towards the goal
- allowing plenty of opportunity for positive feedback from colleagues or clients
- having a good secretary or assistant (with dominant Sensing) who will look after the paperwork, administer the routine jobs, and advise on the practicality of the ENFP's ideas
- seeking to work more in groups than alone

- having an open plan office, with somewhere to retire for privacy, when needed
- undertaking a programme of learning, which is integrated with, and will support, meaningful work

12 ISTJ

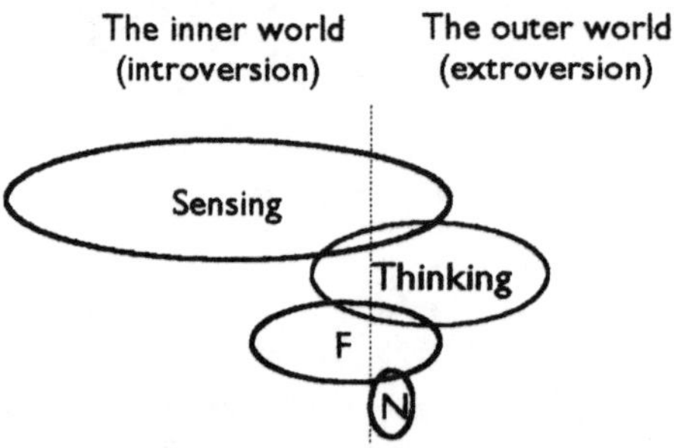

What makes an ISTJ tick?

The Dominant function is the perceptive one of Sensing. Characteristics associated with this function include:

- Likes looking at information in terms of facts and details
- Focuses more on the here and now rather than possibilities for the future
- Feels comfortable in areas of proven experience
- Takes a realistic approach

The perceptive Sensing function is introverted. That is, Sensing is used primarily to govern the inner world of thoughts and emotions. The ISTJ will therefore:

- Seek to develop a realistic understanding of the world as it is, in the light of what he/she observes
- Be pragmatic in nature, constantly learning to adapt to the world as it is now
- Observe in a subjective way, selecting and relating facts that others would not, and seeing those facts more in terms of

impressions and significance than pure fact

The Sensing function is primarily supported by extroverted Thinking judgement, That is, Thinking judgement is used primarily to manage the outer world of actions and spoken words. This will modify the way that the Sensing is directed, by:

- focusing the (inner world) Sensing on impersonal facts and logical options
- tending to spot flaws and injustices
- making decisions on the basis of logical analysis that support the ISTJ's understanding of the world.

The classic temperament of an ISTJ is Epimethean, or Melancholic, for whom a basic driving force is duty, service and the need to belong.

Persuading an ISTJ

Take a style appropriate to the type, as discussed in the chapter on basic interpersonal skills. To turn effective communication into persuasive communication, you should also consider the following points:

- The main currency of communication should be costs and benefits of practical applications
- Show how savings can be made (in quantifiable terms)
- Translate benefits in terms of how they affect the bottom-line
- Don't leave questions unanswered
- If you are not too good on details, have a detailed implementation plan prepared, to avoid giving the impression of being inefficient

You should concentrate on appealing to the ISTJ's dominant function - introverted Sensing. That is, support the ISTJ's (subjective) understanding of the world, and build on those facts the ISTJ sees as significant. It is possible to misunderstand the ISTJ, believe that the extroverted Thinking is paramount, and engage in a logical argument. However, the inward focus on practical objectives, and perception of the world, is more important. Thinking judgement is used in support of this. The ISFJ may therefore:

- appear to change the basis of a logical argument, if the discussion seems to contradict his understanding of the world and works against his personal objectives
- spend more time criticising other's ideas than debating his own - which can lead to the impression of being stubborn.

It is therefore important to encourage the ISTJ to share introverted Sensing thoughts, so that you can find out what his (subjective) understanding of the situation is. You may not be able to dissuade the ISTJ from that subjective impression, and may have to work with it rather than against it. As with all introverts, don't assume that silence means agreement.

Motivating an ISTJ

An ISTJ will find tasks enjoyable or motivating if they involve:

- clarity, e.g.: in communication or objective setting
- clear lines of authority, responsibility and accountability
- a structured working environment, over which the ISTJ can exert control
- privacy to work without interruption
- reward for achievement of the task
- applying experience to practical work
- the ability to achieve goals as a result of hard conscientious work

An ISTJ will find tasks uncomfortable or demotivating if they involve:

- experimenting with something new
- having to accommodate various people's idiosyncrasies
- working with 'soft' issues to do with people - e.g.: insight, growth,
- a high degree of ambiguity about objectives, responsibilities, etc.
- working with large groups
- having to work in an unpredictable environment, over which the ISTJ has little control, and to which he/she has to respond
- working with a lot of ambiguity

Leading an ISTJ

An ISTJ will particularly appreciate a leader who:

- sets clear goals and deadlines that can be achieved using established procedures
- establishes a structured environment with little ambiguity
- is decisive, and fair
- gives praise where praise is due, and criticism where criticism is due
- sets a personal example, that the ISTJ can follow, of being well organised and working hard
- is direct in communication

Contributions to the team of an ISTJ

In a team environment, the ISTJ can contribute by:

- working hard and efficiently to complete tasks by the deadlines

set
- sorting ideas and identifying those that are most practical
- applying a common sense approach to problem solving
- maintaining team focus on the objective
- contributing practical organisational skills
- applying procedures and methodologies
- applying relevant and realistic logical arguments

The potential ways in which an ISTJ can irritate others include:
- focusing too much on the current task at the expense of longer term or interpersonal issues
- not articulating his/her understanding of the situation
- not seeing the wood for the trees
- being too serious
- seeming to be inflexible
- not encouraging others to experiment or innovate
- not promoting his/her own ideas or achievements

As with all types, the ISTJ can achieve personal growth by developing all functions that are not fully developed, through actions such as:
- articulating more of the ISTJ's own views
- developing a long term vision, that avoids focusing on details
- developing a greater understanding of how people feel
- changing things on an experimental basis to see if they can be improved
- learning to promote the ISTJ's ideas and achievements to others, recognising that others may well find them valuable
- making decisions on the basis of how others will feel, rather than objective considerations

Recognising Stress

As stress increases, 'learned behaviour' tends to give way to the natural style, so the ISTJ will behave more according to type when under greater stress. For example, in a crisis, the ISTJ might:
- find a place of solitude in which to think and work
- use tried and trusted means of solving problems
- direct or criticise others' efforts
- use pragmatic solutions at the expense of the long term

Under extreme stress, fatigue or illness, the ISTJ's shadow may appear - a negative form of ENFP. Example characteristics are:
- having a gloomy view of a future

- suggesting impractical ideas
- acting impulsively, and changing things without any thought
- having intense negative feelings towards others (though these might not be expressed)

The shadow is part of the unconscious that is often visible to others, onto whom the shadow is projected. The ISTJ may therefore readily see these faults in others without recognising it in him/her self.

Stress Management

Ways of reducing stress include:

- to recognise and distinguish between one's true preference and learned behaviour, due to cultural, parental or employment demands.
- to structure one's life to allow more use of true preferences

Some ideas for reducing the ISTJ's stress in the workplace are:

- learning to value the contribution that an ISTJ can make in the work situation
- educating colleagues so that they also value the contribution of the ISTJ's true preference
- finding a practical role that involves organising skills
- having a private office or quiet area to work, with access to people when interaction is needed
- the job should have clear, detailed objectives, the achievement of which depend on the ISTJ's own inner resources
- incorporate into the job the acquisition and analysis of information
- have a regular routine
- if the job involves an element of unpredictability, design a procedure for dealing with it
- build contingency into your plans to cater for the unexpected
- use electronic mail, if available, as your usual means of communication

13 INTP

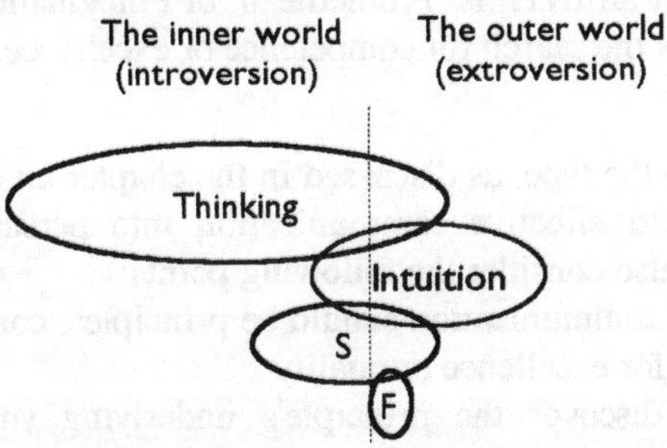

What makes an INTP tick?

The Dominant function is the judging one of Thinking. Characteristics associated with this function include:

- Likes making decisions on the basis of logic, using objective considerations
- Is concerned with truth, principles and justice
- Is analytical and critical, tending to see the flaws in situations
- Takes an objective approach

The judging Thinking function is introverted. That is, Thinking is used primarily to govern the inner world of thoughts and emotions. The INTP will therefore:

- spend time thinking analytically, organising thoughts on a logical basis
- develop an understanding of the principles involved in a situation
- spontaneously feel critical of a person or situation, but not necessarily express that criticism

- be inwardly decisive, but not communicate those decisions to others
- think mostly about impersonal issues, focusing more on concepts, truths and systems rather than individuals' feelings

The Thinking function is primarily supported by extroverted iNtuitive perception. That is, iNtuitive perception is used primarily to manage the outer world of actions and spoken words. This will modify the way that the Thinking is directed, by:

- focusing the (inner world) Thinking on understanding possibilities for the future
- perceiving patterns in information to support the logical analysis

The classic temperament of an INTP is Promethean, or Phlegmatic, for whom a basic driving force is the search for competence or excellence.

Persuading an INTP

Take a style appropriate to the type, as discussed in the chapter on basic interpersonal skills. To turn effective communication into persuasive communication, you should also consider the following points:

- The main currency of communication should be principles, competence and the strive for excellence or quality
- Allow the INTP to discover the principle's underlying your proposal
- Allow the INTP to explore a number of different ideas. Do not settle on an idea, even when suggested by the INTP - the ideas are 'trials' that he/she uses to test the underlying principles. You may find he/she suggests ideas that are later rejected.
- If the criteria (or principles) that the INTP is using to make a decision are not clear, (Thinking is introverted), and you need to know, then ask open questions to find out what they are
- Present costs and benefits in terms of impact on the bottom line, or other objective considerations
- Focus on organisational development and growth, rather than individual issues
- Ensure the presentation is presented competently, and that all assertions are credible

You should concentrate on appealing to the INTP's dominant function - introverted Thinking. That is, support the INTP's logical analysis - get at the truth or principles involved. It is possible to misunderstand the INTP, and believe that the extroverted iNtuition is paramount (e.g.: he has an important vision towards which he is working, or he is driven by a desire to learn and understand). However, there are some core principles, that are paramount and may not be articulated, that take precedence over the extroverted iNtuition. The INTP may therefore appear to be adaptable, flexible and inquisitive until the point when his principles are violated. At this point, the INTP would dig his heels in and surprise everyone at the strength of his stance.

It is therefore important to:

- encourage the INTP to share the principles and criteria that are used by introverted Thinking to make decisions.
- beware of being caught up in the vision of the extroverted iNtuition. These are often prototype ideas, which the INTP is testing out to see whether the results will be consistent with the underlying principles. If the result is not, the ideas and vision can quickly be discarded as other new ideas are tried out.

Motivating an INTP

An INTP will find tasks enjoyable or motivating if they involve:

- intellectual analysis
- suggesting and evaluating ideas
- conceptual discussions about systems, strategies and models
- enabling the organisation to grow and develop
- tackling challenging and complex problems
- improving quality

An INTP will find tasks uncomfortable or demotivating if they involve:

- doing someone else's work
- having to provide a service for others, where there is no requirement for change or improvement
- working in groups
- having to adhere to detailed implementation plans
- being closely supervised
- having to accommodate the feelings of illogical people

Leading an INTP

An INTP will particularly appreciate a leader who:

- gives the INTP autonomy to achieve challenging objectives
- is prepared to debate intellectual ideas to some depth, but leave the final decision to the INTP
- is competent, and respects the competence of the INTP
- recognises and rewards excellence or improvements in quality

- focuses on global outcomes, rather than the detail of implementation

Contributions to the team of an INTP

In a team environment, the INTP can contribute by:

- using analytical and critical skills to solve problems
- focusing attention on the central issue
- providing intellectual insight
- suggesting ideas that achieve long and short term aims
- viewing information objectively

The potential ways in which an INTP can irritate others include:

- being too intellectual
- finding too many flaws, and not accepting imperfect but 'good enough' solutions
- not taking account of others' feelings
- suggesting ideas and then appearing to change his/her mind
- leave others to worry about implementation once the major problems have been solved
- clinging to a principle at the expense of relationships and harmony

As with all types, the INTP can achieve personal growth by developing all functions that are not fully developed, through actions such as:

- expressing appreciation towards others
- working within other people's limitations
- accepting and praising others' imperfect efforts, if they are 'good enough'
- consulting others more, and involving them in decisions, to engender ownership of the solution
- spending time to develop personal relationships for their own sake
- learning to acknowledge and develop the INTP's own emotions and personal values

Recognising Stress

As stress increases, 'learned behaviour' tends to give way to the natural style, so the INTP will behave more according to type when under greater stress. For example, in a crisis, the INTP might:

- withdraw to think about the central issue that needs attention
- suggest various ideas, and use the feedback received to support the intellectual analysis

- debate the issue from an intellectual point of view, and leave it very late before making a decision
- criticise others efforts and ignore their feelings

Under extreme stress, fatigue or illness, the INTP's shadow may appear - a negative form of ESFJ. Example characteristics are:

- expressing intense negative emotions towards others
- being very sensitive to criticism
- becoming preoccupied with details, without any logical basis
- interpreting facts or events in a very subjective way

The shadow is part of the unconscious that is often visible to others, onto whom the shadow is projected. The INTP may therefore readily see these faults in others without recognising it in him/her self.

Stress Management

Ways of reducing stress include:

- to recognise and distinguish between one's true preference and learned behaviour, due to cultural, parental or employment demands
- to structure one's life to allow more use of true preferences

Some ideas for reducing the INTP's stress in the workplace are:

- learning to value the contribution that an INTP can make in the work situation
- educating colleagues so that they also value the contribution of the INTP's true preference
- finding a role that allows the INTP to apply his/her intellectual skill to solve complex problems
- seeking to work alone rather than in groups
- undertaking a programme of learning to increase the INTP's skills and competence
- having a private office, with access to people when needed
- having a good secretary or assistant who will provide practical advice, particularly about how others will feel about the INTP's initiatives, and who will take on some responsibility for the detail of implementation

14 ESFP

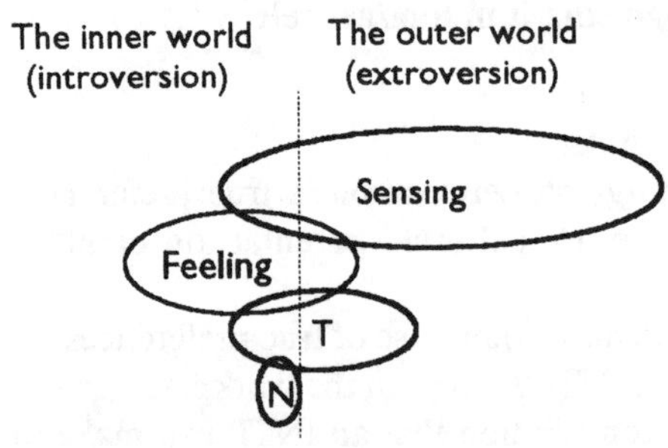

What makes an ESFP tick?

The Dominant function is the perceptive one of Sensing. Characteristics associated with this function include:

- Likes looking at information in terms of facts and details
- Focuses more on the here and now rather than possibilities for the future
- Feels comfortable in areas of proven experience
- Takes a realistic approach

The perceptive Sensing function is extroverted. That is, Sensing is used primarily to govern the outer world of actions and spoken words. The ESFP will therefore:

- Seek to experience and enjoy the world as it is
- Is very responsive to current events, life tending to be a succession of events
- Be pragmatic in nature, constantly seeking to change the world to the way the ESFP wants it to be
- Observe in an objective way, valuing facts without necessarily

putting an interpretation upon them

The Sensing function is primarily supported by introverted Feeling judgement, That is, Feeling judgement is used primarily to manage the inner world of thoughts and emotions. This will modify the way that the Sensing is directed, by:

- focusing the (outer world) Sensing on relationships and facts concerning people
- tending to enjoy action and events for the company of others rather than the events themselves
- leading to enjoyment of interaction with people

The classic temperament of an ESFP is Dionesian, or Sanguine, which seeks to be free from constraint, seeking to enjoy the present, and tending to act on impulse.

Persuading an ESFP

Take a style appropriate to the type, as discussed in the chapter on basic interpersonal skills. To turn effective communication into persuasive communication, you should also consider the following points:

- The main currency of communication should be people, relationships and harmony
- Discuss the practical results for people, especially where it increases the happiness or well-being of the ESFP and those he/she cares about
- Use case studies, ideally with personal references, to illustrate who has benefited to date, and state the benefits explicitly
- Discuss the positive impact on relationships, building harmony, and ensuring everyone's talents are used
- Set your proposal in a personal context and show it provides immediate benefits
- Avoid conflict during your presentation
- Include a substantial element of (purposeful) fun in your proposal so that participants will enjoy it
- Let the ESFP discover how your proposal relates to his/her personal values, and therefore has meaning or purpose

You should concentrate on appealing to the ESFP's dominant function - extroverted Sensing. That is, help the ESFP to discover relevant facts, or enjoy his/her experience of people.

Motivating an ESFP

An ESFP will find tasks enjoyable or motivating if they involve:

- solving urgent problems using proven methods - i.e. fire fighting
- variety, freedom and independence
- a degree of risk
- working with groups
- a fun, action-oriented environment

An ESFP will find tasks uncomfortable or demotivating if they involve:

- no ability to achieve short term objectives - e.g.: only long term research and development of strategy
- the need to stick to pre-defined procedures
- a highly structured environment, using lots of formal meetings
- working with impersonal, paper-based projects, such as book-keeping
- working alone
- being closely supervised

Leading an ESFP

An ESFP will particularly appreciate a leader who:

- sets clear goals and deadlines
- encourages and rewards the taking of risks
- expresses appreciation for his/her efforts
- gives the ESFP headroom to achieve objectives in his/her way
- is efficient, fair, and flexible
- takes a personal and friendly approach

Contributions to the team of an ESFP

In a team environment, the ESFP can contribute by:

- involving everyone in the discussion and decision making
- valuing the strengths of each individual, and encouraging team members to contribute their best work
- using a sense of humour to build a friendly atmosphere
- building a lively 'can-do' atmosphere, which generates team spirit
- focusing on practical ideas
- applying a common sense approach to problem solving
- maintaining awareness of the factual information on which discussions are based

The potential ways in which an ESFP can irritate others include:

- taking too personal a focus - e.g.: taking criticism personally
- acting too quickly, without appearing to think things through
- focusing too much on the current task at the expense of longer

term or interpersonal issues
- not seeing the wood for the trees
- not taking account of costs or logical considerations
- turning to a new problem before the last one has been fully completed
- over-using humour

As with all types, the ESFP can achieve personal growth by developing all functions that are not fully developed, through actions such as:
- developing a greater understanding of how people feel
- stopping and thinking before acting
- ensuring that all aspects of a task have been completed before going on to the next one
- spending time to interpret facts - looking for subjective meaning, and for underlying patterns
- developing time management skills
- establishing a long term goal, developing an outline plan for achieving it, and working towards it
- listing options, and undertaking a formal process of evaluation against criteria, including a cost benefit analysis

Recognising Stress

As stress increases, 'learned behaviour' tends to give way to the natural style, so the ESFP will behave more according to type when under greater stress. For example, in a crisis, the ESFP might:
- draw in other people to help
- use tried and tested methods of solving problems
- act impulsively and take risks
- fail to consider cost implications

Under extreme stress, fatigue or illness, the ESFP's shadow may appear - a negative form of INTJ. Example characteristics are:
- go quiet or withdraw from people
- have a gloomy view of the future
- openly criticise other people
- stop adapting to changing circumstances

The shadow is part of the unconscious that is often visible to others, onto whom the shadow is projected. The ESFP may therefore readily see these faults in others without recognising it in him/her self.

Stress Management

Ways of reducing stress include:

- to recognise and distinguish between one's true preference and learned behaviour, due to cultural, parental or employment demands.
- to structure one's life to allow more use of true preferences

Some ideas for reducing the ESFP's stress in the workplace are:

- learning to value the contribution that an ESFP can make in the work situation
- educating colleagues so that they also value the contribution of the ESFP's true preference
- having an open plan office, with somewhere to retire for privacy when needed
- seeking to work more in groups than alone
- finding a practical role that involves responding to crises - e.g.: fire fighting
- allowing plenty of opportunity for positive feedback from colleagues or clients

15 ENFJ

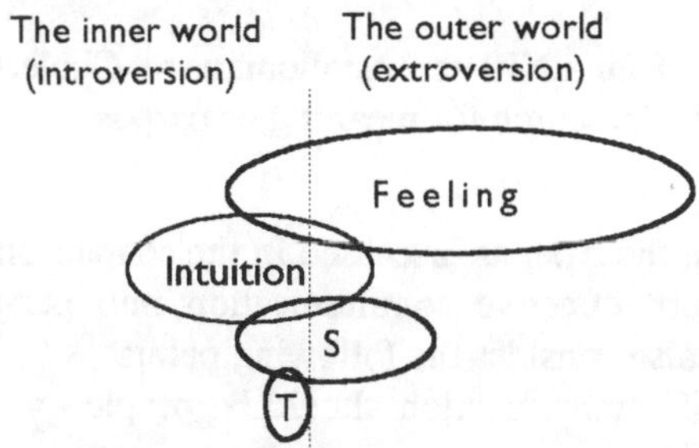

What makes an ENFJ tick?

The Dominant function is the judging one of Feeling. Characteristics associated with this function include:

- Makes decisions on the basis of personal values
- Is appreciative and accepting of people - enjoying company and seeking harmony
- Assesses the impact of decisions on others, being sympathetic or compassionate
- Takes a personal approach

The judging Feeling function is extroverted. That is, Feeling is used primarily to govern the outer world of actions and spoken words. The ENFJ will therefore:

- seek stable, harmonious relationships
- tend to adapt to the environment, taking on board those values that are held as important by friends and family, or society as a whole
- express the appreciation that is felt towards others

- tend to consider others' feelings before his/her own
- be sensitive to praise and criticism, and seek to conform to others' reasonable expectations

The Feeling function is primarily supported by introverted iNtuitive perception, That is, iNtuitive perception is used primarily to manage the inner world of thoughts and emotions. This will modify the way that the Feeling is directed, by:

- focusing the (outer world) Feeling on ideas and possibilities for people
- looking for meaningful relationships
- aiming to understand people, gaining insight into their personality and motivation

The classic temperament of an ENFJ is Apollonian, or Choleric, for whom a basic driving force is the search for meaning or purpose.

Persuading an ENFJ

Take a style appropriate to the type, as discussed in the chapter on basic interpersonal skills. To turn effective communication into persuasive communication, you should also consider the following points:

- The main currency of communication should be people's value, abilities and contributions
- Discuss the positive impact on people, especially where it facilitates insight, growth and development.
- Include a substantial element of (purposeful) fun in your proposal so that participants will enjoy it.
- Discuss the positive impact on relationships, building harmony, and ensuring everyone's talents are used
- Let the ENFJ discover how your proposal relates to his/her personal values, and therefore has meaning or purpose
- Avoid conflict during your presentation

You should concentrate on appealing to the ENFJ's dominant function - extroverted Feeling. That is, support the ENFJ's values, such as the desire for harmonious relationships and the importance of purpose.

Motivating an ENFJ

An ENFJ will find tasks enjoyable or motivating if they involve:

- innovation and creativity, particularly in changing people for the better
- giving people insight and allowing them to grow
- improving team productivity through realising the potential of

the individual team members
- building relationships and reducing conflict
- working with groups, in an atmosphere of openness and trust
- a structured environment
- giving and receiving appreciation

An ENFJ will find tasks uncomfortable or demotivating if they involve:
- meaningless paperwork
- playing politics or using conflict as a tool to increase performance
- working with costs, and figures rather than people
- working in isolation
- criticising others, especially in a group or with people the ENFJ knows well
- receiving criticism

Leading an ENFJ

An ENFJ will particularly appreciate a leader who:
- builds an environment of friendliness and trust
- establishes an inspiring vision - one with meaning or purpose that the ENFJ can believe in
- puts a high priority on communication, and the involvement of people in decision making
- uses a positive and personal approach - praising, encouraging and building rapport
- acknowledges the ENFJ's uniqueness - allowing opportunity for personal growth

Contributions to the team of an ENFJ

In a team environment, the ENFJ can contribute by:
- promoting insight and common understanding amongst the team
- facilitating discussions, encouraging contributions from all team members by asking questions in a structured way
- seeking to arrive at consensus decisions
- generating team spirit though the ENFJ's own energy and enthusiasm
- focusing on areas of agreement and building on others' proposals
- bringing discussions to positive conclusions

The potential ways in which an ENFJ can irritate others include:
- talking too much
- assuming they know the needs of others - in trying to help them

develop insight, the ENFJ can appear bossy
- avoiding conflict and not giving criticism when it is needed
- taking criticism personally
- focusing so much on interpersonal issues that cost and other impersonal considerations are not adequately addressed.

As with all types, the ENFJ can achieve personal growth by developing all functions that are not fully developed, through actions such as:
- learning to observe and accept the negative aspects of those people they admire
- finding an independent and objective means of verifying their insights about people
- pausing and thinking, encouraging others to articulate their own needs, and using active listening to verify understanding
- undertaking a critical appraisal of a situation or person, and expressing disagreement or criticism when it could be of value to the recipient
- focusing on impersonal details when making decisions
- listing options and undertaking a formal process of evaluation against criteria, including a cost benefit analysis
- establishing a long term goal, working towards it, but being prepared to modify it in the light of experience and developing circumstances
- letting others develop at their own pace

Recognising Stress

As stress increases, 'learned behaviour' tends to give way to the natural style, so the ENFJ will behave more according to type when under greater stress. For example, in a crisis, the ENFJ might:
- get everyone organised
- express appreciation for their efforts
- contribute creative ideas, but overlook current realities
- fail to consider the cost implications

Under extreme stress, fatigue or illness, the ENFJ's shadow may appear - a negative form of ISTP. Example characteristics are:
- being very critical and find fault with almost everything
- doing things to excess - e.g.: eating, drinking or exercising
- asking for irrelevant information
- ignoring others' feelings

The shadow is part of the unconscious that is often visible to others, onto whom the shadow is projected. The ENFJ may therefore readily see these faults in others without recognising it in him/her self.

Stress Management

Ways of reducing stress include:

- to recognise and distinguish between one's true preference and learned behaviour, due to cultural, parental or employment demands.
- to structure one's life to allow more use of true preferences

Some ideas for reducing the ENFJ's stress in the workplace are:

- learning to value the contribution that an ENFJ can make in the work situation
- educating colleagues so that they also value the contribution of the ENFJ's preference
- finding a role that has meaning or purpose, perhaps in the area of development of people, that does not involve politics or significant conflict
- having high level objectives to achieve, with the responsibility for organising people to achieve them
- allowing plenty of opportunity for positive feedback from colleagues or clients
- seeking to work more in groups than alone
- having an open plan office, with somewhere to retire for privacy, when needed

16 ISTP

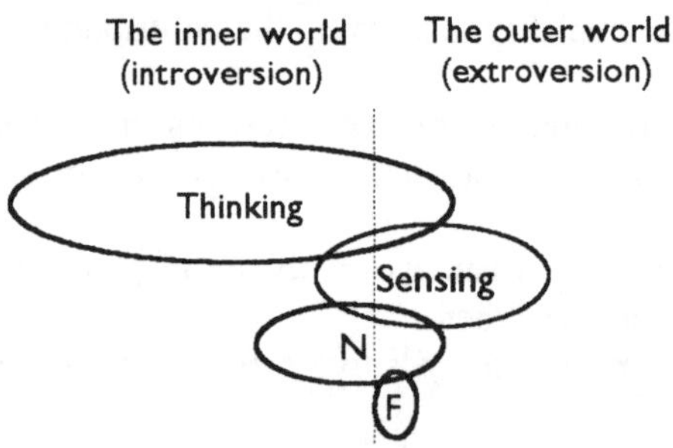

What makes an ISTP tick?

The Dominant function is the judging one of Thinking. Characteristics associated with this function include:

- Likes making decisions on the basis of logic, using objective considerations
- Is concerned with truth, principles and justice
- Is analytical and critical, tending to see the flaws in situations
- Takes an objective approach

The judging Thinking function is introverted. That is, Thinking is used primarily to govern the inner world of thoughts and emotions. The ISTP will therefore:

- spend time thinking analytically, organising thoughts on a logical basis
- develop an understanding of the principles involved in a situation
- spontaneously feel critical of a person or situation, but not necessarily express that criticism

- be inwardly decisive, but not communicate those decisions to others
- think mostly about impersonal issues, focusing more on concepts, truths and systems rather than individuals' feelings

The Thinking function is primarily supported by extroverted Sensing perception. That is, Sensing perception is used primarily to manage the outer world of actions and spoken words. This will modify the way that the Thinking is directed, by:

- focusing the (inner world) Thinking on understanding practical or mechanical problems
- perceiving appropriate facts to support the logical analysis

The classic temperament of an ISTP is Dionesian, or Sanguine, for whom freedom is a basic driving force - seeking to enjoy the present.

Persuading an ISTP

Take a style appropriate to the type, as discussed in the chapter on basic interpersonal skills. To turn effective communication into persuasive communication, you should also consider the following points:

- the main currency of communication should be costs and benefits of practical applications
- describe benefits in terms of how they affect the bottom-line in the short term, and show how these savings can be achieved in practical terms
- discuss logical options
- be prepared for the discussion to jump around from fact to fact
- if the criteria that the ISTP is using are not clear (as Thinking is introverted) then ask open questions to find out.
- describe the steps involved in the process
- don't leave questions unanswered

You should concentrate on appealing to the ISTP's dominant function - introverted Thinking. That is, support the ISTP's logical analysis - get at the truth or principles involved. It is possible to misunderstand the ISTP, and believe that the extroverted Sensing is paramount (e.g.: he has an interest in enjoyment of the present and practical ideas). However, there are some core principles, that are paramount and may not be articulated, that take precedence over the extroverted Sensing. The ISTP may therefore appear to be adaptable, flexible and inquisitive until the point when these inner principles are violated. At this point, the ISTP would dig his heels in and surprise everyone at the strength of his stance.

It is therefore important to:

- encourage the ISTP to share the principles and criteria that are used by introverted Thinking to make decisions.
- beware of being caught up in the ideas of the extroverted Sensing. These are often prototypes, which the ISTP is testing out to see whether the results will be consistent with the underlying principles. If the result is not, the ideas can quickly be discarded as other new ideas are tried out

Motivating an ISTP

An ISTP will find tasks enjoyable or motivating if they involve:

- solving urgent problems using proven methods - i.e. fire fighting
- variety, freedom and independence
- a degree of risk
- clear objectives
- clear communication in factual form
- applying experience to practical work

An ISTP will find tasks uncomfortable or demotivating if they involve:

- experimenting with something new
- having to accommodate various people's idiosyncrasies
- working with 'soft' issues to do with people - e.g.: insight and growth
- no ability to achieve short term objectives - e.g.: only long term research and development of strategy
- the need to stick to pre-defined procedures
- a highly structured environment
- being closely supervised

Leading an ISTP

An ISTP will particularly appreciate a leader who:

- sets clear goals and deadlines
- encourages and rewards the taking of risks
- is direct in communication
- gives the ISTP headroom to achieve objectives in his/her way
- is efficient, fair, and flexible
- gives praise where praise is due, and criticism where criticism is due

Contributions to the team of an ISTP

In a team environment, the ISTP can contribute by:

- being a source of information, or an 'expert' in some subjects
- using analytical skills to produce practical solutions to difficult problems
- encouraging the team to think, and then act
- having a cool head in a crisis
- applying relevant and realistic logical arguments
- encouraging the team to realistically assess the situation

The potential ways in which an ISTP can irritate others include:

- focusing too much on the current task at the expense of longer term or interpersonal issues
- not seeing the wood for the trees
- not completing a task before moving on to the next one
- not communicating his/her understanding of the situation
- taking shortcuts
- seeming to flit from one thing to another

As with all types, the ISTP can achieve personal growth by developing all functions that are not fully developed, through actions such as:

- taking time to consider the impact of the ISTP's approach and ideas on people's feelings
- expressing appreciation towards others
- consulting others, to engender ownership of the solution
- learning to acknowledge and develop the ISTP's own emotions and personal values
- developing a long term personal strategy
- developing personal relationships for their own sake

Recognising Stress

As stress increases, 'learned behaviour' tends to give way to the natural style, so the ISTP will behave more according to type when under greater stress. For example, in a crisis, the ISTP might:

- withdraw from people, to think through possible solutions
- use tried and trusted solutions to short-term problems
- criticise others efforts and ignore their feelings
- sort out detailed points that could perhaps wait

Under extreme stress, fatigue or illness, the ISTP's shadow may appear - a negative form of ENFJ. Example characteristics are:

- displaying intense feelings towards others, or insisting on things being done without any logical basis
- being very sensitive to criticism

- having a gloomy view of the future
- attributing unrealistic negative meaning to others actions or statements

The shadow is part of the unconscious that is often visible to others, onto whom the shadow is projected. The ISTP may therefore readily see these faults in others without recognising it in him/her self.

Stress Management

Ways of reducing stress include:

- to recognise and distinguish between one's true preference and learned behaviour, due to cultural, parental or employment demands.
- to structure one's life to allow more use of true preferences

Some ideas for reducing the ISTP's stress in the workplace are:

- learning to value the contribution that an ISTP can make in the work situation
- educating colleagues so that they also value the contribution of the ISTP's true preference
- finding a practical role that involves responding to crises - e.g.: fire fighting
- having a private office in which to work, with access to people when needed
- seeking to work more alone than in groups, or with things rather than people
- using electronic mail, if available, as a usual means of communication

17 INTJ

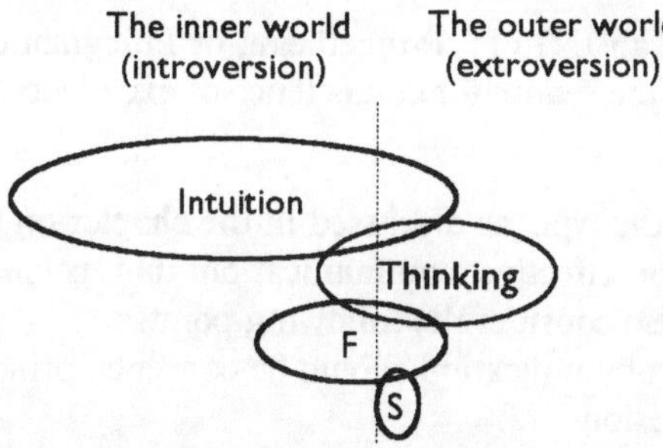

What makes an INTJ tick?

The Dominant function is the perceptive one of iNtuition. Characteristics associated with this function include:

- Likes looking at information from a global viewpoint, spotting patterns and relationships, that lead to an understanding of the key issues
- Focuses more on possibilities for the future than the here-and-now
- Enjoys change, challenge, and variety

The perceptive iNtuition function is introverted. That is, iNtuition is used primarily to govern the inner world of thoughts and emotions. The INTJ will therefore:

- Seek to develop a understanding of how the world can be
- Seek to understand the patterns underlying his/her observations
- Be strategic in nature, wanting to establish a clear vision towards which the INTJ is working
- Not involve others in the development of that vision

The iNtuition function is primarily supported by extroverted Thinking judgement. That is, Thinking judgement is used primarily to manage the outer world of actions and words. This will modify the way that the iNtuition is directed, by:

- focusing the (inner world) iNtuition on ideas and possibilities that relate to systems and concepts
- inwardly maintaining a long term vision. Rather than communicating this vision directly, it may tend to surface in the form of criticism of ideas and situations that do not conform.
- applying logical analysis to perceived patterns and possibilities, enabling the INTJ to quickly see the underlying principles in a situation

The classic temperament of an INTJ is Promethean, or Phlegmatic, for whom a basic driving force is the search for competence or excellence.

Persuading an INTJ

Take a style appropriate to the type, as discussed in the chapter on basic interpersonal skills. To turn effective communication into persuasive communication, you should also consider the following points:

- The main currency of communication should be concepts, principles, possibilities and vision
- Discuss the theoretical aspects of your proposal, and any research undertaken, to open up discussion on the principles involved
- Let the INTJ discover the key principles or issues that underlie your proposal
- If INTJ's vision, ideas or view of possibilities is not clear, then ask open questions to find out what they are
- Discuss a broad range of possibilities for the future, and show how your proposal can help achieve the INTJ's vision or support his/her strategy
- Ensure the presentation is presented competently, and all assertions are credible, and show how your proposal will increase quality

You should concentrate on appealing to the INTJ's dominant function - introverted iNtuition. That is, support the INTJ's vision, ideas, and enthusiasm. It is possible to misunderstand the INTJ, and believe that the extroverted Thinking is paramount (e.g.: logical evaluation of options, cost benefit analysis etc.). However, the inward vision that may not be articulated is more important, and Thinking judgement is used in support of this. The INTJ may therefore:

- appear to change the basis of argument when the logical conclusion is incompatible with the INTJ's vision or understanding of the world
- appear to stubbornly defend an impractical position (whilst the INTJ may view him/her self as open to all arguments). This is because in the outer world, the INTJ spontaneously criticises, whilst in the inner world the INTJ is flexible, and prepared to change his/her views. However, the INTJ rarely involves others in this introverted iNtuitive process and the more flexible side of the INTJ may therefore not be seen.

These points underline the importance of:

- finding out what the INTJ's vision is, and not simply engaging in a (sometimes futile) logical argument
- encouraging the INTJ to share introverted iNtuitive thoughts, so that you can contribute to the formulation of the vision

Motivating an INTJ

An INTJ will find tasks enjoyable or motivating if they involve:

- innovation and creativity, particularly in developing systems, strategies and models
- enabling the organisation to improve and develop towards an ideal
- tackling challenging and complex problems, particularly those that require the development of strategy
- having plenty of privacy, and working with intellectually challenging, competent and strategically minded people
- developing a better understanding and new insights into the way that the organisation works
- task focus rather than people focus
- high level objectives, where the style of delivery is in the hands of the INTJ

An INTJ will find tasks uncomfortable or demotivating if they involve:

- doing someone else's work
- providing a personal, responsive service to people
- having to follow a strict agenda, particularly if someone else has set it
- personal growth exercises
- no requirement for change or improvement

- being closely supervised
- working in a group of people who are not highly skilled

Leading an INTJ

An INTJ will particularly appreciate a leader who:

- gives the INTJ autonomy to achieve challenging objectives that require the development and implementation of an innovative strategy
- is competent, and respects the competence of the INTJ
- focuses on global outcomes, rather than the detail of implementation
- has a strong intellect, and is prepared to discuss and address issues fundamental to the achievement of the vision

Contributions to the team of an INTJ

In a team environment, the INTJ can contribute by:

- challenging the status quo
- leading the team to a greater understanding of the concepts and principles involved
- finding ways to overcome apparently insurmountable difficulties
- developing and maintaining a sense of direction in the team's work
- observing and understanding the way the organisation works, and leading the team to take appropriate action
- producing work to a high level of quality
- ensuring that ideas and vision are translated into action

The potential ways in which an INTJ can irritate others include:

- being single-minded or stubborn
- not taking sufficient account of current realities
- not expressing appreciation for the contributions of others, particularly where it hasn't been fully competent
- not delegating
- making errors of fact, and appearing to make decisions irrespective of the facts

As with all types, the INTJ can achieve personal growth by developing all functions that are not fully developed, through actions such as:

- articulating the INTJ's vision, and allowing others to contribute to its development
- expressing appreciation for work done, even when it falls short of the INTJ's personal standards

- investigating the facts, and documenting them, before interpreting what they mean
- taking time to consider the impact of the INTJ's approach and ideas on people's feelings
- looking for and acknowledging positive contributions and areas of agreement, rather than just seeing flaws and areas of disagreement

Recognising Stress

As stress increases, 'learned behaviour' tends to give way to the natural style, so the INTJ will behave more according to type when under greater stress. For example, in a crisis, the INTJ might:

- retire to a private place and think through a problem until the INTJ has formulated a complete plan for solving it
- try to maintain a high degree of quality in the solution
- criticise others' ideas, particularly if they involve compromising quality
- make errors of fact, or pursue ideas that are unrealistic

Under extreme stress, fatigue or illness, the INTJ's shadow may appear - a negative form of ESFP. Example characteristics are:

- doing things to excess - e.g.: eating, drinking or exercising
- acting very impulsively, perhaps starting off more projects than the INTJ could hope to accomplish
- expressing emotions in an intensive and uncontrolled way
- being very sensitive to criticism
- asking for lots of information that is irrelevant

The shadow is part of the unconscious that is often visible to others, onto whom the shadow is projected. The INTJ may therefore readily see these faults in others without recognising it in him/her self.

Stress Management

Ways of reducing stress include:

- to recognise and distinguish between one's true preference and learned behaviour, due to cultural, parental or employment demands.
- to structure one's life to allow more use of true preferences

Some ideas for reducing the INTJ's stress in the workplace are:

- learning to value the contribution that an INTJ can make in the work situation
- educating colleagues so that they also value the contribution of

the INTJ's true preference

- finding a role that allows the INTJ to increase his/her own competence and achieve new levels of excellence
- having high level objectives to achieve, with a flexible agenda. This provides the freedom to achieve the goals in the INTJ's own way, probably by establishing a vision, developing a strategy, and then implementing his/her own plan.
- have a good assistant who will advise on the practicality of the INTJ's ideas and give feedback on how people feel
- have a private office, with access to people when necessary
- allowing plenty of opportunity for intellectual debate - perhaps by having a mentor

18 ESFJ

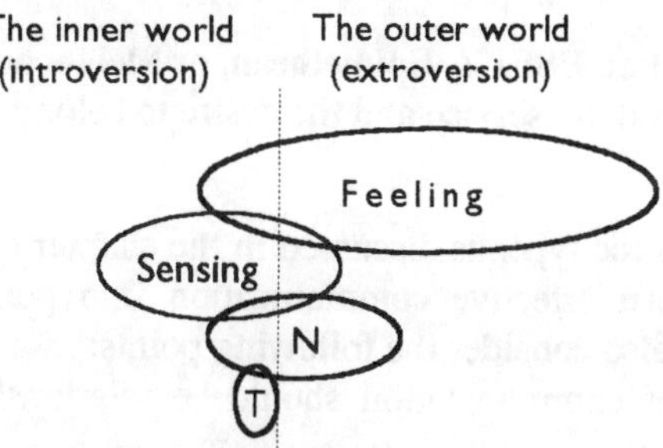

What makes an ESFJ tick?

The Dominant function is the judging one of Feeling. Characteristics associated with this function include:

- Makes decisions on the basis of personal values
- Is appreciative and accepting of people - enjoying company and seeking harmony
- Assesses the impact of decisions on others, being sympathetic or compassionate
- Takes a personal approach

The judging Feeling function is extroverted. That is, Feeling is used primarily to govern the outer world of actions and spoken words. The ESFJ will therefore:

- seek stable, harmonious relationships
- tend to adapt to the environment, taking on board those values that are held as important by friends and family, or society as a whole
- express the appreciation that is felt towards others

- tend to consider others' feelings before his/her own
- be sensitive to praise and criticism, and seek to conform to others' reasonable expectations

The Feeling function is primarily supported by introverted Sensing perception, That is, Sensing perception is used primarily to manage the inner world of thoughts and emotions. This will modify the way that the Feeling is directed, by:

- focusing the (outer world) Feeling on current relationships and people, e.g.: through social events and fact-based conversation
- finding practical ways to be of service to people
- viewing people subjectively, observing facts that support harmonious relationships

The classic temperament of an ESFJ is Epimethean, or Melancholic, for whom a basic driving force is duty, service and the desire to belong.

Persuading an ESFJ

Take a style appropriate to the type, as discussed in the chapter on basic interpersonal skills. To turn effective communication into persuasive communication, you should also consider the following points:

- The main currency of communication should be relationships, harmony and service
- Discuss the practical results for people, especially where it helps the ESFJ and those he/she cares about
- Use case studies, ideally with personal references, to illustrate who has benefited to date, and state the benefits explicitly
- Discuss the positive impact on relationships, building harmony, and ensuring everyone's talents are used
- Set your proposal in a personal context and show it provides immediate benefits
- Avoid conflict during your presentation

You should concentrate on appealing to the ESFJ's dominant function - extroverted Feeling. That is, support the ESFJ's values, such as the desire for harmonious relationships and service to people.

Motivating an ESFJ

An ESFJ will find tasks enjoyable or motivating if they involve:

- helping people and seeing them derive pleasure from the service
- working with people on a regular basis, especially where there is a social dimension
- applying experience to practical work

- giving and receiving appreciation
- compiling information about people
- the ability to achieve goals as a result of hard conscientious work

An ESFJ will find tasks uncomfortable or demotivating if they involve:

- experimenting with something new
- conceptual discussions and analysis
- criticising others, especially in a group or with people the ESFJ knows well
- receiving criticism
- working with costs, and figures rather than people
- working in isolation
- a high degree of ambiguity about objectives, responsibilities, etc.

Leading an ESFJ

An ESFJ will particularly appreciate a leader who:

- sets clear goals and deadlines that can be achieved using established procedures
- establishes a structured environment with little ambiguity
- communicates well, and in a predictable manner
- praises and encourages, and is visibly pleased when the work is accomplished
- is sociable and friendly
- sets a personal example, of being well organised and working hard, that the ESFJ can follow
- has a clear sense of personal responsibility, adhering to personal values of integrity, respect, punctuality, consideration, etc.

Contributions to the team of an ESFJ

In a team environment, the ESFJ can contribute by:

- working hard and efficiently to complete tasks by the deadlines set
- ensuring that everyone in the team feels valued, and that their needs are met
- maintaining good relationships, and building team spirit, often through enthusiastic organisation of social activities
- keeping the team informed, asking for contributions from all members, and seeking to arrive at consensus decisions
- maintaining respect for established hierarchies and traditions
- striving to ensure that people are happy with the service provided

The potential ways in which an ESFJ can irritate others include:

- talking too much
- assuming they know the needs of others
- avoiding conflict, and not giving criticism when it is needed
- not paying attention to their own needs
- not seeing the wood for the trees
- being reluctant to try out new things or work towards new possibilities

As with all types, the ESFJ can achieve personal growth by developing all functions that are not fully developed, through actions such as:

- learning to observe and accept the negative aspects of those people they admire
- trying to view people in a more independent and objective way
- pausing and thinking, encouraging others to articulate their own needs, and using active listening to verify understanding
- undertaking a critical appraisal of a situation or person, and expressing disagreement or criticism when it could be of value to the recipient
- establishing a list of the ESFJ's personal needs, and ensuring they are met - recognising that there are ways in which the ESFJ and others can have both sets of needs met
- establishing a long term goal, working towards it, but being prepared to modify it in the light of experience and developing circumstances
- listing options and undertaking a formal process of evaluation against criteria, including a cost benefit analysis

Recognising Stress

As stress increases, 'learned behaviour' tends to give way to the natural style, so the ESFJ will behave more according to type when under greater stress. For example, in a crisis, the ESFJ might:

- work hard to complete pre-defined tasks
- express appreciation for everyone else's efforts
- fail to recognise the need for change
- neglect their own needs whilst being concerned for others

Under extreme stress, fatigue or illness, the ESFJ's shadow may appear - a negative form of INTP. Example characteristics are:

- being very critical and finding fault with almost everything
- having a pessimistic view of the future
- suggesting ideas that are quite impractical

- ignoring others' feelings

The shadow is part of the unconscious that is often visible to others, onto whom the shadow is projected. The ESFJ may therefore readily see these faults in others without recognising it in him/her self.

Stress Management

Ways of reducing stress include:

- to recognise and distinguish between one's true preference and learned behaviour, due to cultural, parental or employment demands
- to structure one's life to allow more use of true preferences

Some ideas for reducing the ESFJ's stress in the workplace are:

- learning to value the contribution that an ESFJ can make in the work situation
- educating colleagues so that they also value the contribution of the ESFJ's true preference
- finding a role that enables the ESFJ to be of service to people
- having clear, detailed objectives to achieve, with established ways of meeting them
- allowing plenty of opportunity for positive feedback from colleagues or clients
- allowing someone else to be responsible for managing change, who will implement it only when necessary and with sensitivity
- seeking to work more in groups than alone, with people the ESFJ knows well
- having an open plan office, with somewhere to retire for privacy, when needed

19 ENTJ

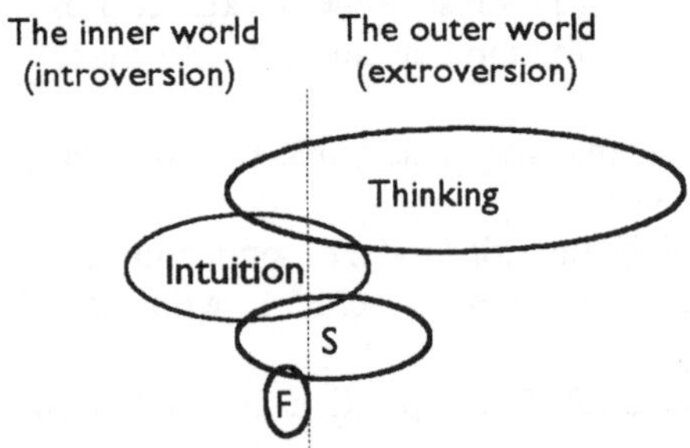

What makes an ENTJ tick?

The Dominant function is the judging one of Thinking. Characteristics associated with this function include:

- Likes making decisions on the basis of logic, using objective considerations
- Is concerned with truth, principles and justice
- Is analytical and critical, tending to see the flaws in situations
- Takes an objective approach

The judging Thinking function is extroverted. That is, Thinking is used primarily to govern the outer world of actions and spoken words. The ENTJ will therefore:

- organise life in on a logical basis, classifying, ordering, and directing facts and situations
- be decisive, with the aim of being just and fair
- spontaneously criticise
- be comfortable with conflict as a way of resolving problems
- take an impersonal approach, focusing more on systems and

organisational needs than each individuals' feelings

The Thinking function is primarily supported by introverted iNtuitive perception. That is, iNtuitive perception is used primarily to manage the inner world of thoughts and emotions. This will modify the way that the Thinking is directed, by:

- focusing the (outer world) Thinking on creative decisions that lead to change and new possibilities
- orchestrating the outward organisation in support of some overall purpose or strategy

The classic temperament of an ENTJ is Promethean, or Phlegmatic, for whom a basic driving force is the search for competence or excellence.

Persuading an ENTJ

Take a style appropriate to the type, as discussed in the chapter on basic interpersonal skills. To turn effective communication into persuasive communication, you should also consider the following points:

- The main currency of communication should be principles, competence and the strive for excellence or quality
- Discuss the costs and benefits associated with your proposal
- Present a series of options, but let the ENTJ decide what should happen and how
- If the overall goal that the ENTJ is working towards is not clear (iNtuition is introverted), and you need to know, then ask open questions to find out what they are
- Focus on organisational development and growth
- Ensure the presentation is presented competently, and that all assertions are credible

You should concentrate on appealing to the ENTJ's dominant function - extroverted Thinking. That is, support the ENTJ's desire to organise and direct change.

Motivating an ENTJ

An ENTJ will find tasks enjoyable or motivating if they involve:

- organising and directing, particularly the implementation of strategy
- conceptual discussions about systems, strategies and models
- enabling the organisation to grow and develop
- tackling challenging and complex problems
- improving quality

An ENTJ will find tasks uncomfortable or demotivating if they involve:

- doing someone else's work
- no requirement for change or improvement
- being closely supervised
- working in isolation

Leading an ENTJ

An ENTJ will particularly appreciate a leader who:

- gives the ENTJ autonomy to achieve challenging objectives
- is competent, and respects the competence of the ENTJ
- recognises and rewards excellence or improvements in quality
- is available to discuss relevant aspects of implementation as and when the issues arise
- focuses on global outcomes, rather than the detail of implementation
- gives the ENTJ a broad portfolio, with the ability to extend it further

Contributions to the team of an ENTJ

In a team environment, the ENTJ can contribute by:

- focusing on the task to be achieved and keeping the team on track
- providing a drive to complete the task on time and to a high quality
- shaping the team structure to best serve the team objectives
- using analytical and critical skills to solve problems
- ensuring short term tasks are in harmony with the strategy
- sorting out confusion and ambiguity
- involving people who are competent in relevant skills, and ensuring everyone knows what they have to do

The potential ways in which an ENTJ can irritate others include:

- issuing directives sometimes without explaining the reasons why
- dominating the team
- not taking account of others' feelings
- driving too hard
- deciding too quickly and without sufficient consultation with others
- not taking sufficient account of current realities
- introducing too much change, and not leaving well-established, workable routines alone.

As with all types, the ENTJ can achieve personal growth by developing all functions that are not fully developed, through actions such as:

- pausing and thinking, and recognising that others will accept the ENTJ's direction if their own contributions are accepted and valued
- working within other people's limitations
- taking time to consider the impact of the ENTJ's approach and ideas on people's feelings
- expressing appreciation towards others
- consulting others more, to engender ownership of the solution
- learning to acknowledge and develop the ENTJ's own emotions and personal values
- spending time to develop personal relationships for their own sake

Recognising Stress

As stress increases, 'learned behaviour' tends to give way to the natural style, so the ENTJ will behave more according to type when under greater stress. For example, in a crisis, the ENTJ might:

- take command, decide what needs to be done, and tell everyone what to do
- maintain a sense of direction, and drive others hard to overcome any short term difficulties
- make decisions too quickly, and without considering the impact on people
- criticise others efforts and ignore their feelings

Under extreme stress, fatigue or illness, the ENTJ's shadow may appear - a negative form of ISFP. Example characteristics are:

- withdrawing and wanting to be alone
- having intense emotions, that may or may not be expressed
- being very sensitive to criticism
- acting very impulsively, doing things to excess

The shadow is part of the unconscious that is often visible to others, onto whom the shadow is projected. The ENTJ may therefore readily see these faults in others without recognising it in him/her self.

Stress Management

Ways of reducing stress include:

- to recognise and distinguish between one's true preference and learned behaviour, due to cultural, parental or employment demands.

- to structure one's life to allow more use of true preferences

Some ideas for reducing the ENTJ's stress in the workplace are:

- learning to value the contribution that an ENTJ can make in the work situation
- educating colleagues so that they also value the contribution of the ENTJ's true preference
- finding a role that allows the ENTJ to shape the organisational structure to achieve long term goals
- seeking to work more in groups than alone
- undertaking a programme of learning to increase the ENTJ's skills and competence
- allowing plenty of opportunity for intellectual debate
- having an open plan office, with somewhere to retire for privacy, when needed
- having a good secretary or assistant (with dominant Sensing) who will provide practical advice, particularly about how others will feel about the ENTJ's initiatives

20 ISFP

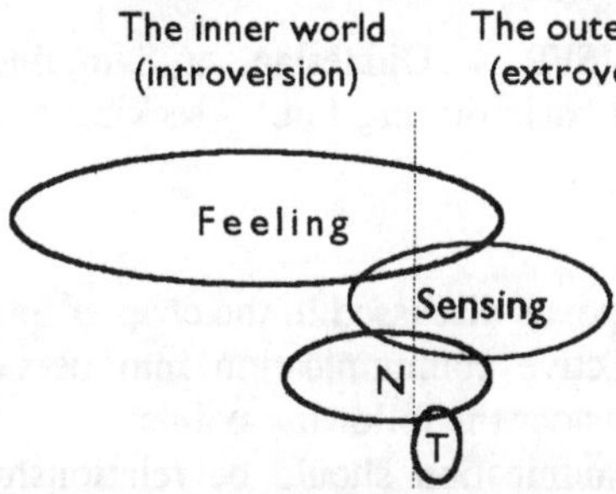

What makes an ISFP tick?

The Dominant function is the judging one of Feeling. Characteristics associated with this function include:

- Makes decisions on the basis of personal values
- Is appreciative and accepting of people - enjoying company and seeking harmony
- Assesses the impact of decisions on others, being sympathetic or compassionate
- Takes a personal approach

The judging Feeling function is introverted. That is, Feeling is used primarily to govern the inner world of thoughts and emotions. The ISFP will therefore:

- develop an inner emotional life that is often unseen to others, but is experienced as intense
- retain a strong sense of values, which are often not expressed
- emotionally accept or reject various aspects of life - for example, deciding whether praise or criticism received is valid and, at

extreme, ignoring whatever is unacceptable
- feel appreciation towards others, but not express it

The Feeling function is primarily supported by extroverted Sensing perception, That is, Sensing perception is used primarily to manage the outer world of actions and spoken words. This will modify the way that the Feeling is directed, by:

- focusing the (inner world) Feeling on current relationships and people, e.g.: through one-to-one discussions and fact-based conversation
- seeking to enjoy the company of those they know, and being concerned for their well-being and happiness
- helping people in practical ways

The classic temperament of an ISFP is Dionesian, or Sanguine, for whom freedom from constraint is a basic driving force - seeking to enjoy the present.

Persuading an ISFP

Take a style appropriate to the type, as discussed in the chapter on basic interpersonal skills. To turn effective communication into persuasive communication, you should also consider the following points:

- The main currency of communication should be relationships and harmony
- Discuss the practical results for people, especially where it increases the happiness or well-being of the ISFP and those he/she cares about
- Use case studies, ideally with personal references, to illustrate who has benefited to date, and state the benefits explicitly
- Discuss the positive impact on relationships, building harmony, and ensuring everyone's talents are used
- Set your proposal in a personal context and show it provides immediate benefits
- Avoid conflict during your presentation
- Include a substantial element of (purposeful) fun in your proposal so that participants will enjoy it
- Let the ISFP discover how your proposal relates to his/her personal values, and therefore has meaning or purpose
- The ISFP may come to conclusions that are not expressed - so ask

You should concentrate on appealing to the ISFP's dominant function -

introverted Feeling. That is, support the ISFP's deeply held values. It is possible to misunderstand the ISFP, and believe that the extroverted Sensing is paramount (e.g.: he has a desire to learn and enjoy life). However, there are some core values, that are paramount and may not be articulated, that take precedence over the extroverted Sensing. The INFP may therefore appear to be adaptable, flexible and inquisitive until the point when his inner values are violated. At this point, the INFP would dig his heels in and surprise everyone at the strength of his stance.

It is therefore important to:

- encourage the INFP to share introverted Feeling thoughts, so that you can find out what his values are
- not assume that the lack of disagreement implies agreement, as the introverted feeling is both reticent to speak, and wary of conflict.

Motivating an ISFP

An ISFP will find tasks enjoyable or motivating if they involve:

- solving urgent problems using proven techniques - i.e.: fire fighting
- variety, freedom and independence
- helping people to enjoy themselves
- applying experience to practical work
- working face-to-face with people whose company they enjoy

An ISFP will find tasks uncomfortable or demotivating if they involve:

- conceptual discussions and analysis
- criticising others, especially in a group or with people the ISFP knows well
- receiving criticism
- working with costs and figures rather than people
- a structured environment, where competence is paramount
- producing and administering implementation plans, especially where people are regarded as resources rather than individuals

Leading an ISFP

An ISFP will particularly appreciate a leader who:

- establishes objectives that involve solving people problems
- allows the ISFP freedom to act independently
- is responsive, particularly in encouraging and rewarding the taking of risks

- doesn't require adherence to rules, written reports, or attendance at too many meetings
- is direct and honest

Contributions to the team of an ISFP

In a team environment, the ISFP can contribute by:

- solving problems as they arise, especially ones concerning people
- generating team spirit through promoting co-operation, and engendering a quiet sense of fun
- ensuring the well-being of team members
- being accurate and observant about facts, without putting too much interpretation on them
- modelling flexibility - e.g.: suggesting his/her own ideas, but being considerate of others points of view and going with the majority
- paying attention to the people side of the problem

The potential ways in which an ISFP can irritate others include:

- being too concerned with harmony in the group
- not pushing the ISFP's own ideas and contribution enough
- being stubborn over issues the group did not anticipate being a problem
- avoiding conflict and not giving forthright criticism when it is needed
- focusing so much on interpersonal issues that cost and other impersonal considerations are not adequately addressed
- perhaps failing to take a longer term view
- taking people at face value and not recognising underlying motives

As with all types, the ISFP can achieve personal growth by developing all functions that are not fully developed, through actions such as:

- being prepared to declare the ISFP's personal values
- interpreting the facts they observe to reveal hidden meanings
- undertaking a critical appraisal of a situation or person, and expressing disagreement or criticism when it could be of value to the recipient
- establishing a long term goal, developing a outline plan for achieving it, and working towards it
- listing options and undertaking a formal process of evaluation against criteria, including a cost benefit analysis

Recognising Stress

As stress increases, 'learned behaviour' tends to give way to the natural style, so the ISFP will behave more according to type when under greater stress. For example, in a crisis, the ISFP might:

- concentrate on what the ISFP sees as important
- work alone if possible
- act impulsively and take risks
- fail to consider the cost implications

Under extreme stress, fatigue or illness, the ISFP's shadow may appear - a negative form of ENTJ. Example characteristics are:

- being very critical and finding fault with almost everything
- becoming bossy and ignoring others' feelings
- having a very pessimistic view of the future
- see hidden meanings that are not really there

The shadow is part of the unconscious that is often visible to others, onto whom the shadow is projected. The ISFP may therefore readily see these faults in others without recognising it in him/her self.

Stress Management

Ways of reducing stress include:

- to recognise and distinguish between one's true preference and learned behaviour, due to cultural, parental or employment demands.
- to structure one's life to allow more use of true preferences

Some ideas for reducing the ISFP's stress in the workplace are:

- learning to value the contribution that an ISFP can make in the work situation
- educating colleagues so that they also value the contribution of the ISFP's preference
- finding a fire-fighting type of role, that allows the ISFP to work towards short-term rather than long-term goals
- having high level objectives to achieve, with a flexible agenda. This provides the freedom to achieve the goals in the ISFP's own way.
- allowing plenty of opportunity for positive feedback from colleagues or clients
- having a good secretary or assistant who will look after budgetary matters, and administration
- having a private office

21 INFJ

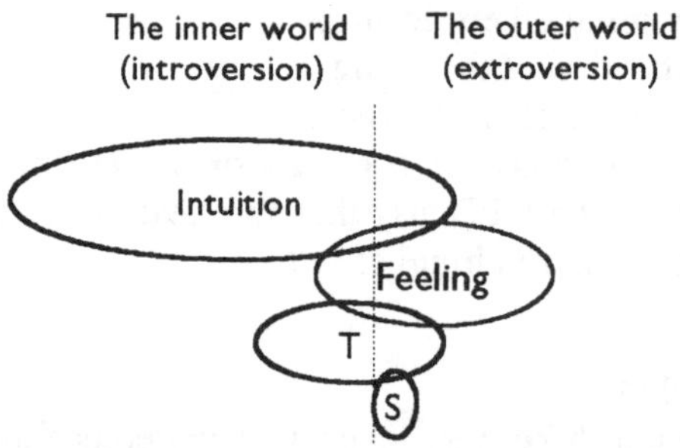

What makes an INFJ tick?

The Dominant function is the perceptive one of iNtuition. Characteristics associated with this function include:

- Likes looking at information from a global viewpoint, spotting patterns and relationships, that lead to an understanding of the key issues
- Focuses more on possibilities for the future than the here-and-now
- Enjoys change, challenge, and variety

The perceptive iNtuition function is introverted. That is, iNtuition is used primarily to govern the inner world of thoughts and emotions. The INFJ will therefore:

- Seek to develop a understanding of how the world is, or can be
- Seek to understand the patterns underlying his/her observations
- Be strategic in nature, wanting to establish a clear vision towards which the INFJ is working
- Not involve others in the development of that vision

The iNtuition function is primarily supported by extroverted Feeling judgement, That is, Feeling judgement is used primarily to manage the outer world of actions and spoken words. This will modify the way that the iNtuition is directed, by:

- focusing the (inner world) iNtuition on ideas and possibilities that relate to people
- expressing appreciation for the contributions of others, particularly where they have done or said something that supports the INFJ's ideals
- making decisions on the basis of values that support the INFJ's understanding of the world, and conform to his/her vision.

The classic temperament of an INFJ is Apollonian, or Choleric, for whom a basic driving force is the search for meaning or purpose.

Persuading an INFJ

Take a style appropriate to the type, as discussed in the chapter on basic interpersonal skills. To turn effective communication into persuasive communication, you should also consider the following points:

- The main currency of communication should be people's value, abilities and contributions
- Discuss the positive impact on people, especially where it facilitates insight, growth and development
- Include a substantial element of (purposeful) fun in your proposal so that participants will enjoy it
- Discuss the positive impact on relationships, building harmony, and ensuring everyone's talents are used
- Let the INFJ discover how your proposal relates to his/her vision, and therefore has meaning or purpose
- If the INFJ's vision is not clear (iNtuition is introverted) and you need to know (as it is the dominant), ask open questions to find out. Such a vision may be difficult to discover if their expression might create conflict in the discussion. The INFJ may be reluctant to share inner thoughts until he/she knows you well.

You should concentrate on appealing to the INFJ's dominant function - introverted iNtuition. That is, support the INFJ's vision, ideas, and enthusiasm. It is possible to misunderstand the INFJ, and believe that the extroverted Feeling is paramount (i.e.: certain values are of paramount importance). However, the inward vision that may not be articulated is more important, and Feeling judgement is used in support of this. The

INFJ may therefore:

- appear to drop values once held as vital, if they start to result in the INFJ's vision being frustrated rather than helped
- appear to agree with a proposition put to the INFJ, but then ignore it in practice - as an INFJ sometimes finds conflict or criticism difficult (both giving and receiving it)

These points underline the importance of:

- finding out what the INFJ's vision is, and not assuming that the lack of disagreement implies agreement
- encouraging the INFJ to share introverted iNtuitive thoughts, so that you can contribute to the formulation of the vision

Motivating an INFJ

An INFJ will find tasks enjoyable or motivating if they involve:

- changing the world and people for the better, particularly in innovative and challenging ways
- giving people insight and allow them to grow
- improving team productivity through a variety of ways
- building relationships and reducing conflict
- working with individuals, particularly in a fun (but not superficial) way
- working in a structured environment, over which the INFJ can exert control
- giving and receiving appreciation

An INFJ will find tasks uncomfortable or demotivating if they involve:

- paperwork that has little purpose
- playing politics or using conflict as a tool to increase performance
- working with costs and figures rather than people
- working with large groups
- having to work in an unpredictable environment, over which the INFJ has little control, and to which he/she has to respond
- establishing hierarchies, divisions of status, or other potential barriers between people
- receiving criticism

Leading an INFJ

An INFJ will particularly appreciate a leader who:

- builds an environment of friendliness and trust
- establishes an inspiring vision - one with meaning or purpose

that the INFJ can believe in
- puts a high priority on communication, and the involvement of people in decision making
- uses a positive and personal approach - praising, encouraging and building rapport
- acknowledges the INFJ's uniqueness - allowing opportunity for personal growth
- gives the INFJ freedom to innovate and is open to his/her ideas

Contributions to the team of an INFJ

In a team environment, the INFJ can contribute by:
- observing and understanding the team dynamics, and encouraging the team to recognise them and take appropriate action
- listening carefully to various viewpoints, and being able to identify potential areas of agreement to be used as a basis to move forward
- being trustworthy, meeting commitments to a consistent standard
- contributing creative ideas, particularly those involving people
- bringing the team to make decisions about important issues
- promoting harmony and co-operation

The potential ways in which an INFJ can irritate others include:
- not including others in the INFJ's process of developing ideas and vision
- not giving criticism or expressing disagreement when it is appropriate
- ignoring current reality in pursuit of insight and meaning - perhaps overlooking some tasks that need to be done
- making errors of fact
- not promoting their ideas in the group
- wanting to pursue ideas without fully thinking through the consequences in, say, cost terms

As with all types, the INFJ can achieve personal growth by developing all functions that are not fully developed, through actions such as:
- being prepared to declare the INFJ's own personal vision or goals
- investigating and recognising the facts before interpreting what they mean
- changing his/her vision to fit more closely with what is possible
- allowing others to participate in the process of development of the INFJ's vision or ideas, in order to gain their commitment or

get a realistic, objective assessment
- learning to promote the INFJ's ideas to others, recognising that others may well find them valuable
- listing options and undertaking a formal process of evaluation against criteria, including a cost benefit analysis

Recognising Stress

As stress increases, 'learned behaviour' tends to give way to the natural style, so the INFJ will behave more according to type when under greater stress. For example, in a crisis, the INFJ might:
- find a place of solitude in which to think and work
- tell everyone else how well they are coping
- try to solve the long term problem, and neglect the short term
- make errors of fact, or ignore routine matters that might nevertheless be essential

Under extreme stress, fatigue or illness, the INFJ's shadow may appear - a negative form of ESTP. Example characteristics are:
- acting very impulsively, making decisions without thinking them through
- doing things to excess - e.g.: eating, drinking or exercising
- being critical of others, and finding fault with almost everything
- being preoccupied about unimportant details and doing things that have no meaning
- acting in a very materialistic and selfish way
- cutting corners, breaking the rules, and even contradicting the INFJ's own values

The shadow is part of the unconscious that is often visible to others, onto whom the shadow is projected. The INFJ may therefore readily see these faults in others without recognising it in him/her self.

Stress Management

Ways of reducing stress include:
- to recognise and distinguish between one's true preference and learned behaviour, due to cultural, parental or employment demands.
- to structure one's life to allow more use of true preferences

Some ideas for reducing the INFJ's stress in the workplace are:
- learning to value the contribution that an INFJ can make in the work situation
- educating colleagues so that they also value the contribution of

the INFJ's true preference

- finding a role that has meaning or purpose, perhaps in the area of development of people, that does not involve politics or significant conflict
- having a private office or quiet area to work, with access to people when interaction is needed
- the job should have high level objectives, and allow the INFJ to provide the inner resources to drive the work forward.
- avoid having too many urgent demands on the INFJ, particularly if they require an immediate response that upsets the INFJ's personal schedule
- allowing plenty of opportunity to give and receive positive feedback to/from colleagues or clients
- find someone who will sensitively advise on the practicality and cost-effectiveness of the INFJ's ideas

22 ESTJ

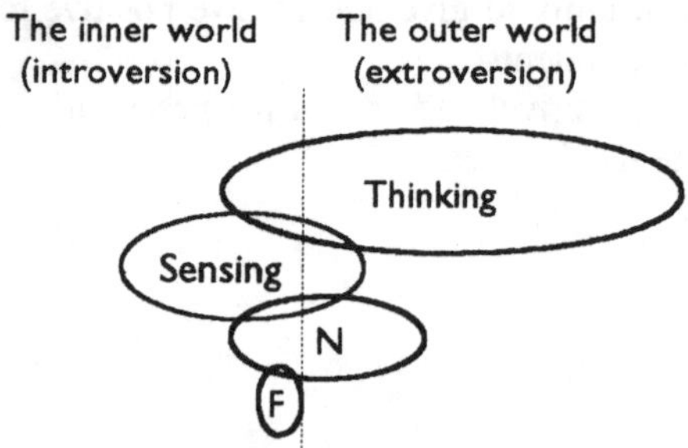

What makes an ESTJ tick?

The Dominant function is the judging one of Thinking. Characteristics associated with this function include:

- Likes making decisions on the basis of logic, using objective considerations
- Is concerned with truth, principles and justice
- Is analytical and critical, tending to see the flaws in situations
- Takes an objective approach

The judging Thinking function is extroverted. That is, Thinking is used primarily to govern the outer world of actions and spoken words. The ESTJ will therefore:

- organise life in on a logical basis, classifying, ordering, and directing facts and situations
- be decisive, with the aim of being just and fair
- spontaneously criticise
- be comfortable with conflict as a way of resolving problems
- take an impersonal approach, focusing more on systems and

organisational needs than each individuals' feelings

The Thinking function is primarily supported by introverted Sensing perception. That is, Sensing perception is used primarily to manage the inner world of thoughts and emotions. This will modify the way that the Thinking is directed, by:

- focusing the (outer world) Thinking on practical decisions that lead to tried and trusted ways of organising or solving problems
- focusing decisions on immediate considerations - e.g.: short term costs and benefits, and the next step

The classic temperament of an ESTJ is Epimethean, or Melancholic, for whom a basic driving force is duty, service and belonging.

Persuading an ESTJ

Take a style appropriate to the type, as discussed in the chapter on basic interpersonal skills. To turn effective communication into persuasive communication, you should also consider the following points:

- The main currency of communication should be costs and benefits of practical applications
- Show how savings can be made (in quantifiable terms)
- Translate benefits in terms of how they affect the bottom-line
- Describe the steps involved in the process
- Don't leave questions unanswered
- If you are not too good on details, have a detailed implementation plan prepared, to avoid giving the impression of being inefficient

You should concentrate on appealing to the ESTJ's dominant function - extroverted Thinking. That is, support the ESTJ's desire to organise and direct action, in familiar territory.

Motivating an ESTJ

An ESTJ will find tasks enjoyable or motivating if they involve:

- clear objectives
- organising and directing, particularly the operation of proven means of solving problems
- clear lines of authority, responsibility and accountability
- a structured working environment, over which the ESTJ can exert control
- clear communication
- reward for achievement of the task
- applying experience to practical work

- the ability to achieve goals as a result of hard conscientious work

An ESTJ will find tasks uncomfortable or demotivating if they involve:

- experimenting with something new
- having to accommodate various people's idiosyncrasies
- working with 'soft' issues to do with people - e.g.: insight, growth,
- a high degree of ambiguity about objectives, responsibilities, etc.
- working alone
- having to work in an unpredictable environment, over which the ESTJ has little control, and to which he/she has to respond
- working with a lot of ambiguity

Leading an ESTJ

An ESTJ will particularly appreciate a leader who:

- sets clear goals and deadlines that can be achieved using established procedures
- establishes a structured environment with little ambiguity
- is decisive, and fair
- gives praise where praise is due, and criticism where criticism is due
- sets a personal example, that the ESTJ can follow, of being well organised and working hard
- is direct in communication

Contributions to the team of an ESTJ

In a team environment, the ESTJ can contribute by:

- working hard and efficiently to complete tasks by the deadlines set
- contributing practical organisational skills
- applying relevant and realistic logical arguments
- calling a spade a spade
- ensuring the team follows through to completion

The potential ways in which an ESTJ can irritate others include:

- focusing too much on the current task at the expense of broader interpersonal issues
- being too blunt in giving criticism
- not seeing the wood for the trees
- not encouraging others to experiment or innovate
- not paying enough attention to others' feelings and values

As with all types, the ESTJ can achieve personal growth by developing all functions that are not fully developed, through actions such as:

- pausing and thinking, and recognising that others will accept the ESTJ's direction if their own contributions are accepted and valued
- working within other people's limitations
- taking time to consider the impact of the ESTJ's approach and ideas on people's feelings
- expressing appreciation towards others
- consulting others more, to engender ownership of the solution
- learning to acknowledge and develop the ESTJ's own emotions and personal values
- spending time alone to develop personal long-term strategies
- spending time to develop personal relationships for their own sake

Recognising Stress

As stress increases, 'learned behaviour' tends to give way to the natural style, so the ESTJ will behave more according to type when under greater stress. For example, in a crisis, the ESTJ might:

- take command, decide what needs to be done, and tell everyone what to do
- use tried and trusted solutions to short-term problems
- make decisions too quickly, and without considering the impact on people
- criticise others efforts and ignore their feelings

Under extreme stress, fatigue or illness, the ESTJ's shadow may appear - a negative form of INFP. Example characteristics are:

- withdrawing and wanting to be alone
- having intense emotions, that may or may not be expressed
- being very sensitive to criticism
- attributing unrealistic negative meaning to others actions or statements

The shadow is part of the unconscious that is often visible to others, onto whom the shadow is projected. The ESTJ may therefore readily see these faults in others without recognising it in him/her self.

Stress Management

Ways of reducing stress include:

- to recognise and distinguish between one's true preference and learned behaviour, due to cultural, parental or employment

demands.
- to structure one's life to allow more use of true preferences

Some ideas for reducing the ESTJ's stress in the workplace are:
- learning to value the contribution that an ESTJ can make in the work situation
- educating colleagues so that they also value the contribution of the ESTJ's true preference
- finding a role that allows the ESTJ to organise and direct, using tried and trusted procedures to solve practical problems
- seeking to work more in groups than alone
- using concrete, achievable targets to measure progress
- providing a service to the organisation, where loyalty is rewarded
- having an open plan office, with somewhere to retire for privacy, when needed
- having a mentor who will listen, and cause the ESTJ to think about the future, take more account of people, and keep his/her options open

Appendix 1
Recommended literature

Gifts Differing

Isabel Briggs Myers (1980)
Consulting Psychologists Press
ISBN 0-89106-011-1

This is the definitive book about Myers Briggs, written by one of the authors of the model and the questionnaire. It goes into detail on the extroverted and introverted forms of the functions, as well as applying Myers Briggs to a number of important areas, such as marriage and learning styles.

Please Understand Me

David Kiersey & Marilyn Bates (1978)
Prometheus Nemesis Book Company
ISBN 0-9606954-0-0

This is a good introduction to Myers Briggs, with particular emphasis on the relationship between Myers Briggs types and the classic temperaments, of which there is much description. Understanding these temperaments better can help to recognise type in others, and identify some of the basic drives that people have.

Navigating Mid-life

Eleanor S Corlett & Nancy B Millner (1993)
CPP Books
ISBN 0-89106-061-8

This book takes a look at the process of maturing that takes place during mid-life. It can help you understand how and why your personality changes as you go through mid-life. If you are experiencing some of the uncertainty, questioning or stress that can occur in mid-life, this book will help you to understand it, and equip you to get through it. It also contains some useful information on the Shadow.

Beside Ourselves

Naomi L Quenk (1993)
CPP Books
ISBN 0-89106-062-6

This book is an in-depth examination of the shadow using Myers Briggs. Recognising your own shadow can be an important aspect of personal development and growth. Through owning it, you will be able to change it. This book will help you to recognise the shadow in your own behaviour.

Appendix 2

Myers Briggs type table

The following pages include a type table for you to populate with the names of people whose Myers Briggs type you recognise.

Myers Briggs type table

ISTJ	ISFJ
ISTP	ISFP
ESTP	ESFP
ESTJ	ESFJ

INFJ	INTJ
INFP	INTP
ENFP	ENTP
ENFJ	ENTJ

Myers Briggs type table